THE MANAGER'S ANSWERBOOK™

Practical Answers to More Than 200 Questions Every Manager Asks

SUSAN BENJAMIN

SOURCEBOOKS, INC.®
NAPERVILLE, ILLINOIS

Published by Sourcebooks, Inc.
P.O. Box 4410, Naperville, Illinois 60567-4410
(630) 961-3900
Fax: (630) 961-2168
www.sourcebooks.com

Library of Congress Cataloging-in-Publication Data

Benjamin, Susan
  Manager's answer book : answers to over 200 questions every manager asks / Susan F. Benjamin.
    p. cm.
  1. Management—Miscellanea. 2. Executives—Miscellanea. I. Title.

HD31.B392 2008
658—dc22

2007050732

Printed and bound in the United States of America.
BG 10 9 8 7 6 5 4 3 2 1

To my agent, Grace Freedson, who makes great books happen.

Contents

Acknowledgments

I have so many people to thank, I'm not sure where to start. Perhaps the best place is with my clients, whose questions, answers, and experience were the fuel for everything in this book. I also got lots of great insights in my interviews with Mary Blake, Martha Boudreau, Mary Beauregard, Paul Condon, Jerry Liebes, Nancy Mills, Steve Sullivan, and, of course, my good friend Ellen Tunstall—thank you all.

Also, big thanks to Sandy Rawdon, whose insights were critical here; Jennifer Homer for training information via ASTD; Donna Lacey for the culture connection; Gloria Hollins, my mentor in deaf culture; and those wonderful women at West Virginia University, Marsa Myers and Chelly Adams, for your great thinking and visionary approach. I also must say thanks to my pals Marie Spadoni and Jen Jones, who have given me valuable feedback about my own, highly personal business.

Thanks of a different sort to the folks at Borders Books, Walden, and Books a Million for supporting authors like me in so many ways, and those many media folks, on TV and radio, for the interviews that help get the word out. As for Peter Lynch at Sourcebooks—thanks, baby, for another book!

And, I would be remiss if I didn't thank my guys, Adam and Dan, for being their glorious selves.

Introduction

Welcome to *The Manager's Answer Book*. This book contains a spectrum of ideas, tools, and inspirations for being a manager—all set up in a Q&A format that targets your most pressing and perplexing questions. But first, let me answer your questions about this book.

Q. What does this book include?

A. This book provides a range of information that should prove helpful whether you're a new manager, still trying to figure things out, or a seasoned manager looking for new insights, new information, and, in some cases, a really good refresher. In the first section, "Attributes of Being a Great Manager," you'll find inspiring ideas about how to maximize your own management potential. As you'll see, you need to tap into your own nature and skill set and find the tools and strategies that work best for you.

The sections "Managing People," "Managing Teams," and "Managing Communications" contain unique approaches to common problems that plague managers. Managers often don't realize just how deeply these issues affect their work lives or the many alternatives available for overcoming them. The final section, "Managing Projects," addresses questions about project management—a nice review for seasoned managers and a great overview if you're new.

Q. How did you determine what questions to answer?

A. I've been working with managers at all levels for almost thirty years. Some of the projects have been large and daunting—especially programs for the federal government whose consequences affect millions of Americans. Others have been small, including four- or five-person start-up operations anxious to take the plunge into success.

So, you can imagine that when my agent asked if I wanted to write an answer book for managers, I was ready to go. I knew the questions and had answered them many times before. Even better, I've witnessed my clients' many failures and successes and have been privy to a range of lessons learned. Of course, no single book can cover all the answers managers need to know, so I had to select from the most prevalent questions and those with answers that are especially hard to find.

While I was writing this book, a wonderful bank of experts provided me with insights into what managers most need to know. Here's who you'll meet:

- Mary Blake is a public health advisor for the Department of Health and Human Services. Mary passed along great insights about the best way to manage a range of work styles, including employees who may have a mental illness. What struck me most about Mary's insights is her belief in the power that all employees have over their work lives and their personal requirements.
- Martha Boudreau is an executive with Fleishman-Hillard International Communications. She provided insights into everything from the best approach to reading books to the surest way to manage an all–type-A employee base. Martha's advice underscores the complexity, and possibilities, of working as a

true team. Perhaps the most pivotal aspect of her approach is an old but eminently true cliché: think—or even better, live—outside the box. To be a great leader, for example, you must be a great follower. To create cohesion in the workplace, try interacting in new ways.

- Mary Beauregard is an intercultural consultant in private practice. The bottom line with Mary is this: we no longer live in a nation. We no longer function in a business. And our way of doing things, whatever that is, no longer exists as the centerpiece of any business interaction. Instead, we live in a world, function as part of that world, and must consider others' perspectives as being as important as ours. In Mary's words, "Managers don't have to adopt, but they do have to adapt."

- Paul Condon is a program director at the Eastern Management Development Center and a former senior organizational development consultant. Among his many responsibilities, Paul is in charge of a comprehensive project management program for managers. What impressed me most about Paul's ideas, and will probably resonate with you, too, is his focus on planning before a project to eliminate a problem later on. You'd be surprised (or maybe you wouldn't be) at how many managers rarely pay adequate attention to this vital requirement.

- Jerry Liebes is the chief learning officer for the Federal Communications Commission. When I interviewed Jerry, I assumed he would recommend training programs that all managers should consider for their employees. What he said was even better: employees and their managers need to determine the right training sessions and vehicles—together. For some, that might mean a seminar on balancing a budget at work. For others, that could mean writing a white paper. The primary consideration, though, is making sure an employee's growth is not canned or prescribed but tailored to an individual and his or her potential contributions at work.

- Nancy Mills, executive director of the AFL-CIO Working for America Institute, provided some helpful answers to how managers can have a healthy relationship with their unions. She had plenty of insights on everything from fairness to pay. The crux of the matter is simple: unions and management have a symbiotic relationship. Healthy and prosperous organizations are great places for employees to work. Healthy and productive employees make organizations great.

- Steve Sullivan is a senior vice president at the Liberty Mutual Group and chairman of the National Association of Advertisers. I've known Steve for quite some time and have long admired his brilliance. In our discussion, what impressed me most was Steve's emphasis on the importance of having an authentic experience at work. This means having a passion for your work, an appreciation of your coworkers, and a solid grounding in doing what's right.

- Ellen Tunstall is a retired executive from the federal government. If you want answers about gender issues or generation gaps, ask Ellen. She's been in the workforce at increasingly higher levels for some time—and is sharp enough to make sense of it. Of all her insights, the most significant to me is how managers must always stay ahead of workplace changes—even the most positive ones—by letting go of old habits and beliefs.

Q. Where should I go if I need more information?

A. Throughout this book, you'll receive plenty of ideas about how to create a learning culture within your department and your own professional life. You'll find book lists and ideas about the best and fastest way to extract information from them; insights into optimal approaches for learning, whether you or your employees are the learners; and websites that contain vast stores of tips and tricks.

Q. How can I reach you if I have questions?

A. You can go to my website, www.susanfbenjamin.com, or email me at susan@susanfbenjamin.com. Don't be shy—I hear from readers all the time. Some have questions, others comment; regardless, all are welcome.

Chapter 1

ATTRIBUTES OF A GREAT MANAGER

1. Visionary

- What exactly do you mean by *visionary*?
- I don't think I am a visionary. I help things along with good ideas, but I don't actually come up with new concepts myself. Where can I start?

2. Risk-Taker

- I worry about everything—from changing the direction on a project to bringing new employees into my team. How can I overcome my apprehension about taking risks?
- I've heard that leaders rely on intuition to help them determine the right direction for managing risks. Can I train myself to become more intuitive?

3. Communicator

- What area of communications should managers focus on most? Writing? Speaking?
- What is the water cooler effect, and how do I avoid it?
- Do I need to be concerned about whether I communicate too often or too infrequently?
- I'm an introvert, so I'm not comfortable speaking, and I don't have time to write. Can I get someone else to communicate for me?
- Should I hire a speechwriter for my presentations?
- What is the best way to tap into my own voice?

4. Organized

- How involved in my employees' projects should I get to make sure my department is organized?
- Like me, most managers need to participate in projects, not just lead the people who work on them. How can I strike a balance between the two?

■ Which do you recommend most—online or offline organizational systems?

■ How about my schedule? Most managers I know have their schedules on the intranet so their employees know when they're available. Is this a good idea?

■ It's hard for me to be organized or adopt a systematic approach when so many fires seem to flare up. Is it possible to plan for surprise problems?

■ Are risk management plans complicated?

■ What else do I need to know about risk management plans?

■ When you talk about human costs, I assume you mean broken legs, head injuries, and so on. But I manage a small consulting firm. Most of our work is in the office, and the biggest threats are things like carpal tunnel and bad backs, which happen gradually. Besides, many of our employees leave after a few years. So, should I add these to my plan?

■ What should I do once I've figured out the costs of these risks?

■ This process seems complex. How labor-intensive does it have to be?

■ Even if you do mitigate the most glaring risks, fires are bound to flare up, right?

■ How can I determine what goes into the contingency plan?

■ What else should I be doing to organize my time?

5. Flexible

■ Why is flexibility so important, especially if I have a solid plan?

■ Obviously, I'd much rather be flexible than reactive. But how do I get that way?

■ I tend to get blocked when I'm under intense deadlines and can't come up with fresh ideas. How can I get the juices flowing?

■ How can I make brainstorming as effective as possible?

■ Should I center brainstorming sessions on a series of specific questions?

■ When should I bring in an outside facilitator?

6. Trusting

■ Why is it so important that I develop a sense of trust?

■ Do you really think it's possible to trust all my employees?

■ How can I tell if a potential employee will fit the mold?

■ I've inherited employees from my predecessor. I feel that they're unreliable and that I shouldn't trust them. Are you saying I should ignore this reaction? Or should I trust my gut?

- Can I delegate the responsibility of recording specific job requirements to a subordinate, such as a team leader, for specific projects or initiatives?
- Can you tell me more about job descriptions?
- If I got more specific, wouldn't the description go on for pages?
- Do you think employees should challenge their responsibilities?

7. Growth-Oriented

- What is the best way for me to grow as a manager?
- What about books?
- Even if I did schedule time to read every day, I'd still get through only a few pages. How can I get enough reading time in to really benefit?
- How about books on tape?
- Are white papers or blogs helpful for managers to read?
- Is it a good idea to attend conferences?
- How do I make sure a conference or training session is worthwhile before I sign up for it?

It's true: All managers have their own style, their own approach to problem solving, and their own way of addressing employees. Good managers know this, accept their limitations to a reasonable extent, and look to their company to fill in for whatever doesn't come naturally to them.

Great managers know this, leverage their strengths to become even stronger, and find resources within themselves to overcome their weaknesses. Do they seek support from the organization? Learn from the experiences of others? Of course. They do so passionately. But they also determine which bits of information, which approaches to problem solving, employee relations, and other managerial duties, suit *them* most as they continue to grow.

So, what attributes do great managers strive to develop? The entire list could fill a book itself, but, without question, the following attributes are key among them.

1. Visionary

Good managers uphold the status quo. They follow directions to the letter. And, in many cases, they inspire employees to maintain their good work. But *great* managers are visionaries who see what no one else can—and inspire the people around them to see it. That fuels energy, excitement, and purpose. In other words, it drives people to succeed beyond their expectations.

Q. What exactly do you mean by *visionary*?

A. Visionaries see the world around them for what it could be. This outlook may apply to specific aspects of the job, such as large projects, or to the general landscape of the company. Regardless, the true visionary has three attributes, and it's well worth identifying these in yourself:

1. You must have a keen eye for possibility, even when things are difficult, risky, or seemingly impossible. You can look through the clutter of the present, with its phone calls, emails, meetings, and demands, and see the potential for your organization.

   Of course, this vision must have a foothold in reality. Anyone can speculate profit margins that break records, a standing in the community that's beyond question, and accolades that come from even the most unlikely places. True visionaries do imagine these things and use them as guideposts as well as a destination.
2. You must have the ability to create plans to help your organization continuously reach its next level of potential. You intuitively gauge the if-only quality, as in "We could become the

leading producer *if only* we had enough capital to invest." Or, "*If only* we had more skilled employees, we could capture that market in the entire region." You allow for a high level of if-onlys because you know that most of them are merely to-do lists you need to fulfill.

Remember, though: if your gut tells you that the if-onlys are insurmountable, listen to it. Look into the reasons why. Then lead your group toward removing those obstacles so you can keep moving. Steve Sullivan, a senior vice president at the Liberty Mutual Group, witnessed his company bolt into the Fortune 100 list and secure an impressive presence worldwide in an amazingly short time. How did they succeed?

Says Sullivan: "At one point, everyone in our universe was heading into broad financial services. But our CEO and president, Ted Kelly, said taking that direction would distract us from our primary objectives. He knew that if you do something really well, you should do more of that." So, Liberty Mutual went against the grain and the company realized huge success. Kelly took risks that were informed by his intuition, his *visionary* ability. But he supported that vision with a deep understanding of the facts.

3. You must be able to communicate your vision with everyone—colleagues, employees, shareholders, and clients—so they not only hear it but also see and experience it on a deeper level. In the process, you'll fuel their energy and excitement. You'll get them talking and thinking about it, giving their input, and finding ways to get closer to it in spite of the obstacles, dips, and curves that naturally spring up along the way. In a sense, a visionary is a master at marketing her vision (more on that in Chapter Four, "Managing Communications").

Q. I don't think I am a visionary. I help things along with good ideas, but I don't actually come up with new concepts myself. Where can I start?

A. If you're not naturally a visionary, you can take two approaches. One is to find experts who complement your skills, including strategists, creative consultants, and brainstorming experts. They'll help you ignite ideas, and if that fails, they'll ignite them for you.

Or, you can rely on your staff. Have meetings that focus specifically on setting a future direction, with the explicit objective of getting great ideas about where the group should be headed and how to get there. Then, apply your intelligence, insights, and leadership strengths to shape and strengthen those ideas. Be sure to let your employees know you value their input. They'll be personally invested in the changes necessary for that vision to become reality and happily manage the disappointments that inevitably crop up.

The second approach is an ongoing one. Consciously seek out inspirations: Read books about great leaders. Learn about new strategies and tactics. Find a mentor or colleague who will help you see things in new ways. It doesn't matter if you've been a manager for five months or fifteen years: you're never too experienced for new perspectives. And push yourself in new directions in your own life: travel to new places, engage in new physical challenges, join discussion groups, or take courses. The newness will help you broaden your perspective and, ultimately, enhance your vision.

2. Risk-Taker

Risks are an important part of any great manager's approach. In essence, risk amounts to this: you *must* keep your unit moving forward, heading in new directions, and testing new approaches. And the reason is clear: the business world is in a constant state of motion. If you aren't growing, you're dying, whether slowly or suddenly, obviously or discreetly. To ensure that your organization is moving in a life-sustaining direction, you must take risks.

Q. I worry about everything—from changing the direction on a project to bringing new employees into my team. How can I overcome my apprehension about taking risks?

A. Try to think of risk as a roller coaster ride. People are either huddled up, clutching the bar for dear life, or sitting high in their seats, arms waving in the air, shouting with enthusiasm and joy. One person is fearful and tight, whereas the other is open and welcoming of every twist, dip, and rise. So, try to adjust your attitude if you can and relish the intensity—and, in the case of business, the possibility—of the ride.

Also, remember that essential quality of balance. Risk has a wildness to it, a high degree of uncertainty. So, balance it with calculations. Look at what facts, anecdotes, and experience—yours and other leaders'—tell you, and stay close to the virtues of good, sound reasoning. That means conducting research before you take risks, particularly risks that could have ripple effects to your employees and/or economic consequences.

You should also be alert to the smaller risks you encounter daily. One of the greatest, potentially most rewarding, and frequently underestimated of them is hiring a new employee. That person poses a financial risk, will shift the dynamic of the group, and will have a ripple effect throughout the workplace. An uncalculated risk means, in essence, that you interview the person, check his or her references, and hire the person. A *calculated* risk means introducing the person to the workforce, testing his or her abilities somehow, talking to several references, and getting input from your other employees. In short, take those steps normally reserved for hiring senior-level employees.

Otherwise, the repercussions can be exhausting and expensive.

This leads to another critical aspect of risk—protecting yourself should the risk not pay off. Most organizations, for example, have a one-year probation period just in case a new employee doesn't work out. Within that time period, they can fire the employee more or less at will.

Other small risks include purchasing equipment, giving presentations (a risk that most managers consider low-key but could have explosive consequences), determining templates for key communications, and requiring safety precautions on the work floor. Will the new, expensive photocopier vastly improve productivity? You should know before you invest.

If your risk involves taking on a new project, be sure to draft a contingency plan so that you'll have an out if the project goes sour. Include finance (where you'll get additional funding, how you'll back up your cash flow), client issues (how to find new clients, how to address dissatisfaction), and solutions to predictable problems (your launch doesn't work, bad PR). The contingency plan can have a psychological effect, also: You'll feel stronger and more inclined to take unusual chances knowing you have a net.

Q. I've heard that leaders rely on intuition to help them determine the right direction for managing risks. Can I train myself to become more intuitive?

A. Because you have so many tasks demanding your attention simultaneously (multitasking) and function in a changeable universe filled with uncertainties, being in touch with your intuition is critical. In our discussion of vision, we looked at Liberty Mutual and its CEO and president's sharp intuition when making decisions for the company's future. Liberty Mutual, of course, is an example of a large-scale success; intuition can help you in smaller decisions, too, even down to scheduling issues.

If you don't think you're naturally intuitive, there are a few things you should know. First, not everyone operates at the same level of intuition. You may be more systematic or rely more on experience than on intuition. Second, you can't "build" or "develop" intuition. Rather, you need to open up the intuition that already lies inside of you. So, unlike developing skills for managing budgets or adhering to policies—which requires you to work hard and acquire knowledge—intuition requires that you let go and stay focused on your inner core.

One common approach is meditation. Although this may sound New Age-y, it's actually rooted in sound business practice. Essentially, you clear the clutter from your mind for twenty-minute intervals, focusing primarily on your breathing and, for some people, a simple sound. In the end, your thoughts will flow more easily and be informed by the subtle powers of your intuition. Try experimenting with different types of meditation until you find the way that works best for you, whether by incorporating existing methods or by finding ones entirely of your devising.

Similar to meditation is visualization: this is where you sit quietly, breathe deeply and regularly, and visualize where you'd like to be. Visualize whatever it is that makes you relaxed and happy, whether it is a tranquil beach setting or a successful ribbon cutting. You can learn visualization techniques through books and articles, an adult education center, or your local gym.

Another critical way to tap into your intuition is obvious yet overlooked: stay fit. In fact, truly great managers know that keeping fit is part of an entire approach to life—one that doesn't settle for mediocre returns or being *almost good* at anything. By caring for your body, you care for your mind and are taking necessary literal and metaphorical steps toward excellence. If you can't engage in a full-fledged exercise routine, you should still eat right, sleep enough, drink in moderation, and take a short walk every day at lunch.

3. Communicator

Josh Stella is a technology geek. He's worked for the federal government, private enterprises, and entrepreneurs on everything from websites to complex systems. So, when I was researching my book *Project Management for Top Performers* (Sourcebooks, 2007), I interviewed Josh. I asked which technology tools he would recommend to managers that could help them better manage their projects. His response surprised me. "They can get all the tools they want, but first they have to learn how to communicate with people. That's where most projects fall apart."

So, I started thinking about my own clients. For most, their problems weren't related to unskilled employees: the skill levels were adequate or more than adequate for the tasks. And it wasn't that their employees were unmotivated; most craved positive outcomes and the rewards that go with them. But a lot of the managers I worked with had trouble communicating critical information to their employees, bosses, customers, and other stakeholders and didn't focus on motivating, rewarding, or, more significantly, leading them.

Yet, amazingly, few managers actually considered communications a core requirement of their own performance. They value the importance of strong writing and speaking skills, especially in light of people's reliance on the language of emails and the web; but they send their employees to training or delegate their speeches or blogs to someone else. Unfortunately, communication-related problems have the potential to haunt you throughout your entire professional life; you use communication skills in every aspect of being a manager, and you need to know how to use them effectively.

Q. What area of communications should managers focus on most? Writing? Speaking?

A. Great managers master communications on all levels. The need for strong writing skills becomes more dire every day because of the business world's reliance on websites, blogs, and emails and their shrinking use of phone calls and one-on-one exchanges. The problems aren't necessarily the result of poor grammar or an overly chatty (and unbusinesslike) voice. Even details or nuances can skew the message and spur a negative response.

For example, say a manager sends this email: "The reports are due by 1:00 today. Failure to meet this deadline will result in project cancellation." Naturally, employees think that if they don't get their reports in by 1:00, the project will be canceled. Yes, they know that the original deadline was three days ahead and the staff hadn't finished their fact-checking. But the email is clear and would certainly lead to panic. As a result, the following scenario could occur:

- Employees get the message.
- They panic.
- They start emailing each other for clarification.
- They meet for water cooler conversations.
- They spread rumors that the project was more tentative than anyone thought.
- They drop other projects to focus on the report.
- They feel demoralized.

If this scene had occurred in a meeting, the entire interaction would have been different. For one, the manager would have used more exact language to make his point, because people—particularly businesspeople—are generally better speakers than writers. He could have contextualized the message, too, so employees would know the circumstances surrounding the issue and why it occurred. If the employees had questions, the manager could immediately address them—before gossip and rumor kicked in.

You may wonder why, if the issue was so important, the manager didn't assemble everyone for a meeting or, at the very least, meet with a few subordinates or project managers who would spread the word. In all likelihood, the message really *wasn't* that important—it only appeared that way because of the manager's poor writing skills.

The employees really didn't need to worry. The manager had a serious problem with the passive voice and omitted critical nouns from his message. Had he bothered to write a thorough, clear email, his message would have read this way: "Our clients' employees must have their reports in by 1:00 today. If they fail to meet this deadline, the client will have to cancel their efforts on the project, and we'll fill in."

This kind of situation may seem extreme, but it isn't. Every day, good managers send unclear or unfocused messages that employees fail to understand, and the water cooler effect kicks in.

Q. What is the water cooler effect, and how do I avoid it?

A. The water cooler represents the parts of the workplace where people gather and chat (it generally isn't around the actual water cooler anymore these days)—in the halls, in the cafeteria, and during chance encounters at intersecting corners of cubicles. Of course, many of those interactions occur in virtual places as well, such as informal emails that get passed on to other employees. As quick and unpolished as these conversations may be, employees actually get a substantive amount of information about work issues there—well over 60 percent, according to some sources.

Unfortunately, much of this information is incorrect, containing varying degrees of truth. Rumors fly, and the employees may get confused, misguided, or demoralized. Yet, water cooler conversations rage on, holding more power than most other communications venues. And the reason? Employees, unable to count on reliable sources of information, seek clarification from their informal networks.

If you feel more comfortable speaking than writing, remember that you still must rely on written communications to empower you as a manager. The reason has much to do with how people receive and process language:

- People hear every third word or so in conversations and during speeches.
- They remember less of what they hear than what they read.
- They remember more when they read and hear the information together.
- People hear what they want—especially what confirms or adds to their beliefs.

So, discussions are critical and can give you the flexibility necessary to address questions and provide context. But they may not stop the water cooler talk from flowing; to really communicate effectively, you need to send important information verbally and through email. People will still gossip, but they may spread more accurate information.

Q. Do I need to be concerned about whether I communicate too often or too infrequently?

A. How much information you send—and when you send it—really does matter (we'll discuss this in greater detail in Chapter Four, "Managing Communications"). Consider these facts:

- The more information you send people, the less attention they pay to it; if you get lots of emails from a particular colleague or employee, you know exactly what I mean. In other words, don't overwhelm them.
- Send emails sooner and not later. For example, if you know that your company is planning an organizational change, don't wait until other departments have heard to tell your employees what the changes entail. By then, that water cooler—and all the anxiety, questions, and misconceptions—will be flowing. Instead, let your employees know new information the minute it's appropriate.
- One of the major causes of workplace (and life) anxiety is feeling out of control. So, if you can't address events that everyone knows are brewing, at least tell your employees that you'll keep them updated the moment you can.
- Because people best retain information they both see and hear, be sure to combine both communications vehicles whenever possible. For example, create an agenda and handouts for all meetings, even short ones. Use a flipchart to record employees' points so participants can retain, and clarify, information. Above all, have someone take minutes and send them out later.

Q. I'm an introvert, so I'm not comfortable speaking, and I don't have time to write. Can I get someone else to communicate for me?

A. Yes and no. No, you can't get anyone to send your emails, run your meetings, or give your client presentations any more than you can get others to anticipate what you want to say. And you can't avoid these forms of communication. But, in some instances, you can rely on other people and a variety of supports to help your communications go quickly and smoothly. Here are a few:

- Use templates. Everything you write, from proposals to objectives for your employees to formal presentations and marketing material, can be boiled down to a template. You can find these online, in books, and in your organization's files. Simply look at the documents that work best and duplicate the order of information, key words, and tone every time you communicate similar messages.

- Take a class. Plenty of executive programs include communications as part of their curriculum. You can find courses specifically geared to helping managers get the results they need at work. Some seminars on spoken communications include videos where you watch yourself speak, whereas written communications courses may focus on everything from emails to complex white papers.

- Find an editor. Your editor can be anyone at work who has a true grasp of the strategic value of communications and can give you feedback about what works and what doesn't. You should also consult your HR department about what employees may interpret as degrading or inappropriate language and avoid this—and make sure your employees avoid it, too.

- Find a facilitator. If you have trouble conducting meetings or leading groups, get a facilitator—and make sure that person gives you tips and techniques you can apply later. Ask about the best approaches given your group's dynamic, and get feedback about your personal style.

- Read. You cannot overestimate the importance of reading—not only as an information source but also as a method for improving your communications. When reading, you naturally internalize the style of the message; and the more you internalize, the more you can duplicate.

Q. Should I hire a speechwriter for my presentations?

A. You can, yes, and plenty of great managers do—almost all U.S. presidents have used speechwriters. But you *still* need to communicate the thrust of your message to that person and review and edit the speech once you get it. So, in other words, you're not off the communication hook.

Q. What is the best way to tap into my own voice?

A. Many managers and their employees struggle with the idea of finding their voice, but, unless you're writing poetry or fiction, you don't need to reach your inner voice and shouldn't use it. Instead, focus on reflecting your organization's voice and getting your employees to do the same. If you can't identify that voice, ask your HR or marketing department if they have a style guide, or work off your organization's ad campaigns. Organizations with fast, spicy ads, for example, can contain fast, spicy language—within the boundaries of professional acceptability, of course.

If your company has no identifiable voice and no ads, or at least no compelling ads, ask your communications department or an outside vendor to help you formulate one. This process may be no more complicated than nailing down the tenors of plain language, or it may involve complex strategies.

4. Organized

Numerous systems, from online organizers to day planners, are available to help managers get organized—so many, in fact, that you practically need organizational skills to organize the systems. Good managers know which ones to pick and choose, and they use them effectively. Great managers know that all the supports in the manager's closet are simply that—supports. Managers alone are the organizational force. In fact, let's look at the difference between good and great managers in this regard:

Good managers address the situations immediately before them with full attention.

Great managers address the situations immediately before them and are aware of how these situations affect the five or ten other situations under their jurisdiction.

Good managers focus on details.

Great managers focus on big-picture issues and delegate responsibility to employees who use their expertise to tend to details.

Good managers check their schedules regularly.

Great managers determine their schedules constantly.

Good managers check in with their employees daily to ensure that everything is on track.

Great managers check in with their employees at intervals so they can focus on other issues.

Your approach to organizing is more than ball juggling: it's integral to your management style and of key consequence to your and your department's growth.

Q. How involved in my employees' projects should I get to make sure my department is organized?

A. Good managers prioritize their tasks and focus on the ones that most deserve their attention. Time plays a critical factor in this hierarchy: the nearer the deadline, the closer they focus. If an important proposal is due in a few days, they zero in on that. But great managers have a different set of priorities altogether, focusing instead on projects that require their involvement. This means they must trust their employees and delegate responsibilities, checking in only at specific times. Is a deadline around the corner? That's inconsequential to their priority list; they should have someone on it whom they trust to do a great job, so they can focus on more important tasks.

This may seem obvious. But you'd be amazed (or maybe you wouldn't) at how many managers don't delegate responsibility, hoard top-level projects to themselves, or burn time with meetings and ongoing check-in sessions with their employees. As a result, they micromanage, overseeing every detail of every project down to the last subhead of a report—which is a waste of their time and their employees' skills.

In any business, every project is composed of hundreds of pieces, most of them so small that you don't think of them until you get there. Micromanaging managers get so snagged in these details that they can't address countless other matters that demand their attention. Questions go unanswered, deadlines float by, and routine matters threaten to flare up into raging fires while the managers' energy and time are consumed by tasks that belong to someone else.

Q. Like me, most managers need to participate in projects, not just lead the people who work on them. How can I strike a balance between the two?

A. That's an excellent question, but once again, the answer lies in your organizational abilities. That means you must be incredibly clear about your responsibilities, those you delegate to other people, and the deadlines and priorities for both.

For most managers, visual supports can help. You can invest in complex software systems or use something as simple as a list in a work journal that helps you track your daily, weekly, and monthly responsibilities.

Another well-known tool that can help save you time and energy is the Gantt chart, a common resource for managers. Most likely, you've seen Gantt charts hundreds of times. They can be used in just about every kind of project, from quick weekend off-sites to six-month research projects. It's been in popular use since American engineer Henry Laurence Gantt invented it in 1917.

You can easily draft a Gantt chart with Excel or Microsoft Project. It's easy to use and helps you focus on tracking tasks and allocating resources. Just put your tasks in one row, at the far end of your chart. Then run dates across the top at increments that make sense to you: days, weeks, or months. If your project is important but has a remarkably short duration, like a weekend, you can even break it down to hours. The horizontal bars indicate the amount of time each task should take. So, your Gantt chart might look something like this:

Tasks	Week 1	Week 2	Week 3	Week 4	Week 5
Send Invitations	▬				
Tally RSVPs		▬			
Rent a Hall		▭			
Buy the Food			▬		
Rent Tables and Chairs			▬		
Assemble a Wait Staff				▬	
Prepare and Serve					▭
Legend					

▬ Meg   ▬ Beth
▬ Jo   ▭ Amy

Whether you're using a Gantt chart or some other organizational system, remember these points:

- Include a reasonable number of tasks—fifteen or twenty is a good place to stop.
- Break down your tasks into main tasks and subtasks.
- Add an extra column indicating who does what so that you can keep track of your employees.
- Make use of visual possibilities—be creative. Here are some ideas:
  - Color-coded bars
  - Thicker or thinner bars
  - Different shapes for the bars, such as straight lines or wavy lines or wavy lines over straight lines, to indicate whatever . . .
  - Inverted triangles to indicate milestones
- Review your chart every few weeks—more often if you need to.

Q. Which do you recommend most—online or offline organizational systems?

A. That depends on the person. Personally, I like the offline journal-like organizers: I carry mine with me everywhere, use different colored inks to delineate priorities, and stash it in my briefcase or top desk drawer when it's not in my hands. It's real, tangible, and ever-reliable, because it doesn't rely on external sources of energy such as electricity or batteries. But most managers spend enormous amounts of time online, and with technology shrinking to pocket-size, you can experiment with several methods and find out what works best for you.

Q. How about my schedule? Most managers I know have their schedules on the intranet so their employees know when they're available. Is this a good idea?

A. Good managers let their schedules be available to administrative assistants, employees, and others in their unit so that their coworkers know where and how to find them. *Great* managers let their schedules be available to whoever needs them, but they also ensure that they're not the first or even second stop should problems or questions crop up.

Instead, great managers establish an infrastructure that contains clearly defined point people, whether supervisors or team leaders, who are capable of answering questions and handling problems. Regardless, these people have the availability and expertise to address issues correctly.

Assign each of your employees a specific area of expertise when other employees or customers have questions. This strategy offers the following benefits:

- People will no longer waste their time by searching for someone to answer their questions—instead, they'll know to go straight to the designated expert.
- People will consistently receive accurate information.
- Your employees will take fuller responsibility for their areas of expertise and related workplace issues.
- People will rely less on the water cooler conversations discussed earlier.

This will benefit your customer service representatives, as well—they'll know exactly where to direct calls for the necessary information.

Q. It's hard for me to be organized or adopt a systematic approach when so many fires seem to flare up. Is it possible to plan for surprise problems?

A. Absolutely. And the best way to do that is to put together a risk management plan in which you identify your risks and determine ways to mitigate, eliminate, or address problems should they occur. This concept applies regardless of your field or enterprise: many managers mistakenly think that addressing risk is necessary only if you're managing a warehouse, a restaurant, a construction site, or any other area with a high potential for physical injury or fatalities. However, all sorts of problems can arise in any business; a contingency plan can help you minimize their damage.

Q. Are risk management plans complicated?

A. They're as complicated as you want them to be. Of course, the more vulnerable your venture, the more detailed the planning you should do, and the more advice you should get from experts. So, for example, a complex construction project in a downtown area needs a solid risk management plan, but so does an ice cream shop where employees are prone to literally backbreaking slips and falls.

Q. What else do I need to know about risk management plans?

A. A risk management plan isolates your risks and helps you analyze and prepare for them. As I mentioned, you'll need to identify your risks first. First, try breaking your risks into categories:

- Human:
  - Difficult to find qualified staff
  - High turnover in employee base
  - Possibility of employees stealing secrets
  - Vulnerability to other forms of theft
- Health and safety:
  - Workplace hazards
  - Security concerns

- Possible injury to customers or employees
- Toxic fumes
- Sales and marketing:
  - Saturated market
  - High cost of marketing and PR
  - Industry or other scandals
- Environmental:
  - Flood zone
  - Toxic landfills near site
  - Environmental risks to area of interest

Once your list is complete, look for details you may have over-looked; many risks will be hidden, so you need to examine your lists carefully. It's also a good idea to review the last few years of business for reoccurring problems that you should plan for in the future. If you're starting a new business or initiative, research the experiences of similar businesses.

Another helpful strategy is to list the most significant tasks your employees perform. Beneath each item, record all the associated risks you can think of. Don't worry about overloading your list or being overly cautious—you can make judgments about what to address or eliminate later. As the saying goes, the devil is in the details: a crack in a levee, a bad product, a small but malfunctioning machine part that injures an employee.

Let's focus on a seemingly simple example: an ice cream shop. The operation may seem straightforward: as long as the freezers work and the customers come, the profits should be decent. In reality, though, the manager needs to consider a whole litany of possible risks, including staff injuries due to slips and falls on wet floors; staff stealing equipment and/or money; potential turnover of staff; break-ins and robberies; suppliers opting out of the deal; competition springing up; and so on.

You'll notice that not all of these risks are equal—next, you need to prioritize. One of the ice cream shop owner's threats might be environmental: a flood, a storm, or other volatile weather could damage the facility, as well as present a good reason for customers to stay home. However, the likelihood of this occurring in most places is relatively low—unless the shop is in a seaside tourist town that's prone to hurricanes.

Now, determine how much the risk will cost in terms of dollars, time, and quality; then estimate the cost of preventing or mitigating the threat and compare it to the cost of enduring it. You might find that preventative measures cost more than actually addressing the problem, should it occur. If that's the case, then the risk isn't truly a risk—it's a nuisance. The only exception is human costs: take all steps necessary to protect your employees from injuries, no matter what.

This is how the manager of our hypothetical ice cream shop might evaluate her risk:

- **Environmental damage.** The manager knows she must purchase extra insurance. A few thousand dollars will cover most environmental hazards—not bad compared to the potential cost of *not* having insurance.

- **Theft.** This risk is likely but preventable—or at least something the manager can control. Remember, the ice cream shop can be robbed, but so can the customers going to and from the parking lot. The cost of mitigating the risk equals the price of an alarm system, floodlights, locks for the windows, and other small expenses.

- **Turnover of staff.** Ice cream shop workers are usually high school and college kids hoping for extra cash to last through the summer. Some may come and some may go, but workers will never be in short supply. The cost to stop this tide could mean a compensation package, higher wages than those offered by equivalent shops, and other amenities that would be nice in a professional venue but not at an ice cream shop.

Q. When you talk about human costs, I assume you mean broken legs, head injuries, and so on. But I manage a small consulting firm. Most of our work is in the office, and the biggest threats are things like carpal tunnel and bad backs, which happen gradually. Besides, many of our employees leave after a few years. So, should I add these to my plan?

A. Yes. You should take every precaution necessary, no matter how long you expect your employees to stay. This issue is less about finance and more about integrity and the responsibility of business owners to create the safest possible workplace for their employees.

But considering human costs also makes good business sense. By recognizing the value of employees and the cost of injuries on their own lives, you plant the seeds for a healthy business culture: one where people thrive and will want to stay. This helps avoid turnover and makes for a happy workforce, which benefits everyone.

Q. What should I do once I've figured out the costs of these risks?

A. Determine the best step forward. If the risk seems likely, you may want to avoid that line of work. Say you want to sell your software program in a new market to boost your company's profits. If you realize that the new market is saturated, and the risk is high, you might scrap the idea and move on. If you're building a retail shop in a high-crime neighborhood, move to a safer area and swallow the additional rent charge.

Or, you might opt to mitigate the risk. For example, the ice cream shop owner could require employees to wear rubber-soled shoes to avoid the hazards of slips and falls on inevitably damp or greasy floors. Or, if you're working on an analysis of some sort for a client, your risk might be that the data you're using aren't sufficiently updated. So, you will mitigate this risk by having an employee double-check your facts.

In many cases, you can also transfer the risk. For example, if the manager of the ice cream shop had a lease and did not own the building herself, she could negotiate with her landlord to repair damages should a storm occur because of "acts of God." If she owned the building, she could rely on her insurance policy. Transferring risk won't stop the worst from happening but can help if it does.

Finally, accept that the risks are possible, but prepare and hope for the best.

Q. This process seems complex. How labor-intensive does it have to be?

A. As I've said, you need to prioritize your risks depending on your line of work: you want to have financial means and a plan for anything that will seriously jeopardize your solvency or cause bodily harm to anyone. Also, remember that new projects and challenges constantly bubble up. You may need to address risks on an ongoing basis—not dozens all at once.

It can help to compile this information on a graph of some sort so that you and your stakeholders can see it quickly and easily. If your risks are not highly complex, draw a simple chart that has a column for each risk, the cost of mitigating it, and the value of addressing it. Then assign a numerical value to each of them: 1 being the lowest priority and 10 being the highest. Address everything with a high score and table the rest.

For example, the ice cream shop risk management chart might

look like the following:

Most   Least
10 —————————————————————————————— 1

Risk	Likelihood	Costs	Relative value of addressing the risk	Score	Decision
Robbery/drugs	7	9	9	25	Mitigate
Staff turnover	10	0.5	0	10.5	Ignore
Injuries from slips and falls	5	9	9	23	Mitigate and transfer

For more complex projects, you can rely on one of the many technology tools available for risk management.

Q. Even if you do mitigate the most glaring risks, fires are bound to flare up, right?

A. Right. Fires always occur (due to cash flow crises because clients don't pay, employees who drop the ball, etc.), and it's your job to put them out. As with your risk analysis—where you identify the risk—the contingency plan provides measures you can take should these fires occur. For example, if cash flow is a concern, your contingency plan may include setting up a line of credit or starting an emergency fund. Make new contingency plans each time you begin a new project or whenever there's a change in company processes. For example, say you're adding new technology to the workplace. Make sure everything is backed up *and* have a plan should the tool encounter glitches.

Your contingency plan may have these qualities:

- **Employee networks.** What if a problem hits and you can't make it to the office? Do you have a way of reaching your employees so they know what to do next? What to expect? How to keep the work cycle flowing? Make sure your employees know whom to reach and how—whether by phone, email, or a quick trip to that person's desk.

- **Technology backups.** Technology can fail you in a number of ways, from emails that don't go through to an afternoon when your website falls offline. Your contingency plan must address all of these potential failures; it should include a work-from-home plan so key employees can remain productive, directions on how to retrieve backup files and software, and the names and numbers of necessary tech support personnel.

- **Alternative facilities.** You may need alternative facilities for any number of reasons: your warehouse may get flooded, your facility destroyed, or your street clogged because of a community event. You need to address these, among other, questions: Where will you house your merchandise? How will you keep it from spoiling? Where will your employees work and still have access to your company's data? You should identify names and numbers of nearby storage units and warehouses and draft relocation plans.

Q. How can I determine what goes into the contingency plan?

A. Take a what-if approach by asking yourself what-if questions, such as, "What if our warehouse becomes unusable?" It's a good idea to involve your team, especially when you're engaging in a new project. You ask the question and let them answer with a worst-case scenario. So, you might ask:

"What if . . . we couldn't get supplies on schedule?"
"What if . . . we can't use our facility?"

Put each of these scenarios into one column. Then, in a separate column labeled "Then we . . . ," write the solutions—the essence of your contingency plan. Sometimes, the solutions may be obvious; other times, you'll need to investigate. If you're concerned about your computers crashing, for example, bring in an expert who can recommend backup measures. Here's how your chart might look:

What if . . .	Then we . . .
. . . we can't get supplies?	. . . contact the Chicago warehouse and have them store supplies for us.
. . . we can't use the facility?	. . . follow the emergency work-from-home plan.

Q. What else should I be doing to organize my time?

A. There are numerous strategies for time management, but more important than finding a strategy is that you look at your personal management style and figure out what works for you. Among other questions, ask yourself these:

- How is my style unique?
- What seems to get in the way of my being organized?
- What approaches am I using now that I can adapt or replace?
- In what situations have I been the most organized as a manager, and why was that possible?
- What do I need, in terms of products or people, to help myself and my department become better organized?

By the way, if you find an organization system or strategy that you like, don't be afraid to adapt it to suit your style. No one right model exists for *anything* in the business world—you need find the options that work best for you and manage them according to your style.

5. Flexible

Every manager eventually struggles with unexpected surprises that occur for unknown reasons. As a result, you must take a rubber-band approach and remain flexible. This does not conflict with being organized; in fact, you can be flexible only if you are organized. Otherwise, you'll just be applying one quick fix after another, chasing one fire after the next. This will cause you, and your employees, incredible misery and angst.

Q. Why is flexibility so important, especially if I have a solid plan?

A. Even with the best plan, you must be flexible enough to address the setbacks or changes that may hit you unexpectedly, including the following:

- Shifts in finance
- Canceled projects
- Employee issues, from managing attrition to quickly ramping up staff
- New opportunities that demand your time
- Downturns in the market
- Upturns in business that create sudden volume
- Personal problems—yours or an employee's

One or all of these issues will derail your projects, shift your priorities, and otherwise affect your life as a manager—not once, but countless times. In any of these situations, though, there's a difference between being flexible and being reactive. Look at the difference:

Reactive: You rush around, talk to people, and try to figure out what to do next.

Flexible: You gather information, develop a plan, and draft a priority list for everyone involved to follow.

Reactive: You pull people from projects.

Flexible: You reassign people to new projects.

Reactive: You hold impromptu meetings with whatever supervisors or team leaders are available.

Flexible: You contact supervisors or team leaders about changes through a predetermined method of communication.

Reactive: You let a few people know of the changes because there isn't enough time for everyone else. Besides, they'll hear about it somehow.

Flexible: You make sure that supervisors or team leaders alert their employees about the change, and then you address hanging questions or concerns at the next all-staff meeting.

Q. Obviously, I'd much rather be flexible than reactive. But how do I get that way?

A. If you feel you're not flexible, rethink the idea of flexibility. Yes, it can be a character trait, but it can also be a logistical approach. Try to stop yourself when you start reacting to roadblocks and examine your past responses. For example, say you need to add new employees for an unexpected project. In the past, you may have gone through the usual channels, starting with an ad in the newspaper. But the response may have been too slow.

Instead, pull back and write a list of alternatives. These may include hiring a search firm, sending out an email asking your employees for recommendations, or finding temporary help to pick up lower-level tasks so that your existing employees can be more productive as you search for new hires. Remember that your habit will be to react in the most familiar, but not necessarily the optimal, way. So, you will need to apply *conscious* thought to this process—a hard task when you're rushing but one that will pay off in the long run.

Q. I tend to get blocked when I'm under intense deadlines and can't come up with fresh ideas. How can I get the juices flowing?

A. Brainstorming can be really helpful, not only with your employees or colleagues but also when you're alone. In fact, brainstorming helps train your mind so you can quickly and instinctively think in new ways in a variety of situations. Here are some steps you should take:

- Sit in a quiet room with a piece of paper and a pen. You can use your laptop or computer, of course, but the connection between the words and the thought will be closer if you actually handwrite.
- Write your mission at the top of the page.
- Make a numbered list from 1 to 10. This will give you guidelines about the number of ideas you must put down, no matter how blocked or empty you feel.
- Write your ideas—don't quantify, qualify, or second-guess. Just write. Where possible, write quickly: the faster you go, the less likely it is that you'll mull through the negatives and the better your ideas will ultimately become. Be as solution-driven and positive as possible.
- You may get stuck around the end of the list. If so, think up the most outrageous possibilities and keep going.

- Once you're absolutely sure you've written every single idea, write three more. Believe me, they'll come. But, once again, don't monitor or second-guess. Your true potential for creativity and innovation may surface at this point.
- Put the list aside and do something else.
- Return to the list and cut the least likely possibilities, and then focus on the ideas that are left. At this point, you may want to get feedback from a colleague, a boss, or an employee. In fact, you could use your best ideas to spur brainstorming sessions with them.

Q. How can I make brainstorming as effective as possible?

A. To hold a brainstorming session for your employees, start by organizing a meeting in a quiet room with at least two flipcharts and plenty of brightly colored markers. By the way, flipcharts are better than whiteboards, because you can save the pages as you go. And remember: the visual component of brainstorming plays a significant role in your success. Make sure everyone can see the flipcharts and understand your writing.

Begin by outlining the rules of the brainstorming session. For example, no one can mock, mimic, or otherwise interfere with another person's thinking. They can't criticize each other's ideas but can build on them or replace one idea with a better one. Also, be clear about the time frames—let them know exactly how long the brainstorming component of the meeting will take and stick to that limit.

Write the matter you want to address on a flipchart at the front of the room. Be sure to be as forward-looking and positive as possible. For example, say you manage a small software development practice and want to position your new tool in the market. You would write "Determine ways to position tool in the market" and not "Do we have ways to position the tool?" or, even worse, "Find solutions to the problem [or challenge] of how to position tools in the market." By giving your employees a forward-looking direction, they're more likely to take an energetic and positive approach.

Begin the brainstorming. How you start really depends on the group, the issue you're brainstorming, the complexity of that issue, and your own style.

Generally, though, this approach works well:

- Ask employees to write ten ideas on a piece of paper. This will give them ideas to work with throughout the discussion—especially useful for introverts or shy employees.
- Let employees talk through their ideas. They can read from their lists or just go off the tops of their heads.
- Write ideas on a flipchart as they arise. Ask questions of employees' ideas to fuel the discussion, or quickly add an encouraging comment if an idea is especially impressive.
- Do not stop for discussion, fine-tuning, or disagreements. Just keep the energy flowing.
- Return to the list and review each of the items. Cross out the ones that seem the least helpful. Don't worry about hurting anyone's feelings: with all the ideas that surfaced, no one will remember, or care, who was responsible for what.
- Narrow down the ideas to one or two, and then work up a plan for addressing each.
- End the session when the ideas or time runs out.

If the energy is flowing and the enthusiasm is running high, don't end the session. You don't want to miss out on good ideas. However, tell your employees that you're running late and set a limit for the additional time you'll take. If the brainstorming session is one part of a larger meeting, this shouldn't be a problem. But if you're spilling into time that has been dedicated to other projects, you may need to excuse one or two employees who can't stay.

Q. Should I center brainstorming sessions on a series of specific questions?

A. This concept is great if you have multidimensional issues to discuss or simply too many details to address in one simple brain dump. Remember: the purpose of the brainstorming session is not to outline specific tasks or strategies but to find big-picture solutions. Still, when a great idea strikes, and the group is inspired, it's fine to get into the weeds.

As with any brainstorming session, start by assembling your employees in a quiet room with two flipcharts, some markers, and an agenda. Bring a list of questions that you drafted beforehand, starting with the five Ws—who, what, when, where, and why—and, when applicable, how. You don't have to use all five Ws, but you should use some of them as you lead the discussion. You don't have to share these with anyone; just use them to keep yourself on task. For example, you might ask the following:

- What is the unique aspect of our product?
- What separates it from our competitors' products?
- What approach has worked well in positioning products like ours in the past?

The *who* questions could look something like this:

- Who are our primary targets?
- Who on the team is most familiar with our target audience's needs?

You can deviate from these questions throughout the brainstorming session depending on the answers you get. If the group is dynamic and the contributions come quickly and easily, you can push for more targeted or specific ideas. So, your conversation might work something like this:

> *You:* What is unique about our tool?
> *Them:* It helps our client work faster.
> *You:* Our tool does do that—but so does our competitor's. So, what is really unique?
> *Them:* It combines the benefits of earlier versions.
> *You:* Name the three top benefits they appreciate given the feedback you've received.

Once you have their input, you've entered the most creative and satisfying part of the brainstorming session. Start by crossing out redundant responses, and then cluster the remaining ideas into groups by content. You may have ideas that don't seem to fit or things employees think of suddenly at this stage. Don't intimidate or inhibit them—just put them on a separate flipchart page, or some other so-called parking lot, and review them later. By the way—remember the two flipcharts I mentioned earlier? Use one for their comments and the other for the parking lot ideas.

Next, weed out the good ideas from the great ones—you could have participants vote for whatever they think works best. This type of brainstorming has the potential to result in specific answers to your most pressing questions; just this little bit of structure can do a lot.

Q. When should I bring in an outside facilitator?

A. If the subject is highly contentious, the content seems personal, or you don't have the knowledge or skills to address pertinent issues, consider using an outside, neutral facilitator. You can probably find one through your HR department or by asking your colleagues for referrals.

A good facilitator draws on the participants' existing knowledge or ideas—even if the participants forgot they had them. This happened to me at a recent session that I facilitated for an organization whose mission was to develop a curriculum for supervisors and managers so they could keep pace with the company's growth. In only two hours, they created a mission for the program, a framework for courses, and an approach for winning executive-level buy-in. The ideas seemed to spring out of them—not because I, the facilitator, planted them, but because I stepped back far enough so they could grow.

6. Trusting

In a culture built on competition, where businesses steal ideas and employees are said to be searching for the next best thing, trust may seem like an anomaly at best—and a bad idea at worst. In reality, though, trust should rank high on the list of attributes that you strive for. In fact, trust is at the core of what makes good managers great. It's neither amorphous nor emotional but a management style built on sound strategy and approaches.

Q. Why is it so important that I develop a sense of trust?

A. Trust is the foundation of your most critical activities as a manager. One obvious example is when you delegate responsibility—you can succeed only if you trust the employees to fulfill their tasks and resist second-guessing or micromanaging them to distraction. Otherwise, you'll create a whirlwind of problems. For example, you may be spending too much time thinking about your employees' tasks instead of focusing on your own.

Paul Condon, a program director at the Eastern Management Development Center and former Organizational Development consultant, puts it this way: "There's a pat phrase that says a manager should do only those things that they're good at and delegate the rest. That way, you maintain the focus where it should be."

In addition, Condon points out that untrusting managers cheat their employees out of a valuable career opportunity. "People who work for you must grow and develop as decision makers, too. By delegating to them, even in complex or unusually difficult projects, you're giving them an opportunity to extend themselves professionally and grow." The payoff for everyone—organization, employee, and manager, who now has a stronger, more well-rounded employee—is enormous.

Perhaps one of the most deeply hidden drawbacks, though, is this: untrusting managers damage employee morale. In essence, they say that employees aren't good enough to do the job themselves. And this soon becomes a self-fulfilling prophecy. But, if you delegate and trust they'll do a good job, they'll rise to the occasion and even surpass it.

Q. Do you really think it's possible to trust all my employees?

A. Good managers know the difference between blind trust and trust. With blind trust, they haphazardly delegate responsibilities to all employees, regardless of each person's skill set, experience, or personality. Good managers recognize the amount and type of responsibilities individual employees can handle and then delegate accordingly. The drawback to this approach is that weaker employees never get a chance to excel and the stronger ones tend to be overloaded with work. But the job gets done.

Great managers unite the workforce so it grows as a team. They spend time creating a mission and vision statement, which they share with their employees to win their buy-in and ignite their loyalty and energy. But they do more than *write* these statements: they live by them, referring to them consistently and using them as clear guidelines for their department. (We'll talk more about mission and vision statements in Chapter Three.)

When hiring new employees, great managers have no ambiguity about the requirements of the job, the team, and the department's mission. These requirements aren't tucked away in their brains— they are on paper, revealing themselves in the job descriptions, strategic plans, and even the many duties that are part of every project management plan.

Q. How can I tell if a potential employee will fit the mold?

A. You don't want a "mold"—you want clear, unambiguous criteria that candidates can adapt to in their own unique way. Obviously, you'll look for other important factors in their personality, work style, and, of course, specific aspects of their experience. Here's some advice:

Don't: Use old job descriptions or templates that someone in the company produced years before.
Do: Create new job descriptions with input from your employees about the qualifications that serve your overall department best.

Don't: Go through the typical interview process of bringing the prospect in for a round of interviews.
Do: Bring the prospects in for a round of interviews, and then invite them to stay to meet and ask questions of your employees.

Don't: Contact their referrals for general information about the employees' performance and then read between the lines.

Do: Have discussions with the employees' referrals, being careful to ask specific and highly targeted questions to help inform the decision.

Q. I've inherited employees from my predecessor. I feel that they're unreliable and that I shouldn't trust them. Are you saying I should ignore this reaction? Or should I trust my gut?

A. Every manager has faced this struggle since the beginning of commerce. You can't fire employees at will, nor do you want to—it causes stress and ignites insecurity in your entire team. Besides, laws governing the workplace ensure this can't occur.

Instead of forcing unreliable performers out, try tapping their strengths and maximizing their weaknesses. As we mentioned, good managers recognize their employees' strengths. Great managers know that their weaknesses (outside of substance abuse or other remarkably negative behaviors) can actually benefit the organization.

For example, a client at a research organization where I consulted needed to keep the workforce updated about the constant changes that bubbled up throughout the company. One of her employees, Gerry, posed a threat to this mission. She was unpleasant to work with, sabotaged projects by spreading rumors, and introduced processes that slowed them down. Naturally, she alienated everyone working on support projects, from executives to contractors. My client was stuck. Gerry had been an employee for many years and wasn't about to leave, even with a buyout offer. Besides, the department had important work to do and not enough people to do it, and there was a marginal chance that the organization would fill slots once they were open.

Fortunately, my client had the presence of mind to work off Gerry's weaknesses and put them to good use. She assigned Gerry, a former manager, the task of coordinating projects online, a job that required little face-to-face contact. Gerry had no input into the content, no say over timing, and no employees to manage. Yet, she had complete control over her area of responsibility and had the professional satisfaction of knowing she was at the hub of activity.

Whether you have employees like Gerry or not, it's critical that you define each employee's responsibilities clearly in terms of his or her expected contributions to projects and to the group. Many managers take this step lightly: they tweak old descriptions, address the most general requirements, and rely on conjecture to determine responsibility. In short, they don't focus enough on determining how to leverage their employees' skill sets.

You also need to articulate and record these expectations. Depending on your style and the complexities and demands of your department, you have a few options. One is to develop a traditional job description—usually a compact paragraph or two. This document serves numerous functions: it tells individuals about their specific responsibilities and the outcomes you expect of them, clarifies your expectations of contractors or suppliers, serves as an agreement between you and your employees (although not legally binding), and informs team members about the best source of knowledge for particular project-related issues.

Q. Can I delegate the responsibility of recording specific job requirements to a subordinate, such as a team leader, for specific projects or initiatives?

A. You can delegate this responsibility—but make sure that the person taking over for you recognizes what's involved and carefully and clearly connects team members with their tasks. In fact, this is a great time for you to act as a consultant, providing feedback about their choices.

Q. Can you tell me more about job descriptions?

A. Just about every workplace has job descriptions for their employees. Most touch on a range of responsibilities and some get into the very specific tasks of a position, but these documents most often provide general job direction or indicate culpability should mistakes occur. This is an example from a hospital job description:

> Must check in with patients on a regular basis and address their individual needs. This person is also responsible for tracking the patients' progress and sending any changes to the appropriate authority.

This leaves many questions unanswered. For example, "regular basis" could mean once a week or once an hour. As for "appropriate authority," that could mean anyone—a nurse, a nurse practitioner, the physician-in-charge, or the patient's family. Most likely, this sort of description wouldn't pass legal review in a lot of hospitals or health care units. A clean, clearly articulated description, however, will eliminate ambiguity:

> Must check in with patients every hour, more as required, to check vital signs, dispense medication, and inquire as to how the patients feel. They should record their findings on the patients' health charts, indicate their progress, and send any changes to the doctor-in-charge.

If you don't have specifics, at least provide a range. For example, you could say, "Check in with patients every sixty to ninety minutes," or reference a document that provides more in-depth information: "Check in with patients at regular intervals, as defined in the Hospital Handbook, Section 4.2."

Q. If I got more specific, wouldn't the description go on for pages?

A. Not at all. You should cluster the tasks and record those that encompass other, smaller ones. For example, you would say, "Must check their vital signs . . . ," but not, "Must take their temperature, check their blood pressure, listen to their heart . . ." All those smaller tasks are implicit.

Q. Do you think employees should challenge their responsibilities?

A. Some managers believe that criticism fosters negativity, but actually, openness is critical to creating a culture of trust. As long as employees have opportunities to voice their opinions, they won't find surreptitious ways to work against you. What's critical is that you provide the right venues so they can speak out as professionally and constructively as possible. Some managers favor suggestion boxes, whereas others opt for meetings where they address comments that employees have submitted anonymously.

The best option, and the frequency of these communications, depends on your group and, as we've been saying all along, your personal style. Regardless, take their concerns seriously. Your employees have a unique vantage point that can inform your decisions and provide you with a context you might otherwise miss. Listening to their concerns also validates their position as integral to the department and affirms that they are people worthy of trust. They will undoubtedly respond in kind.

7. Growth-Oriented

Anyone who stops learning is old, whether at twenty or eighty. Anyone who keeps learning stays young.

—Henry Ford

Good managers are experts at their jobs. They consistently do them well and encourage their employees to do the same. In essence, they're maintainers who don't rock the workplace boat and can be counted on to head in a clear, unwavering direction year after year. But great leaders are on a perpetual path to growth. They keep ahead of the trends and are curious and exuberant about the possibilities of something new. They take on more risk and are much more likely to lead their employees to great success.

Q. What is the best way for me to grow as a manager?

A. Many managers, no matter how overwhelmed with deadlines, still find the time to work out, even if that means getting up extra early or sandwiching their workout routines between meetings. I know of one university president who devotes time to Iron Man training.

Approach your professional growth time in the same way. Find a time every day to research a new finding in your field, or take fifteen minutes every day just to sit and think about your challenges and your mission. In fact, thinking is one of the most underestimated aspects of managing. It requires nothing more than sitting at a quiet café or on the commuter rail in the morning. It does mean putting away Blackberries, cell phones, and other distractions: even if you don't think you'll get any calls, you need to wipe away any remote possibility of interruptions.

Q. What about books?

A. Books are a tremendous source of information that will spur your growth and motivate and inspire you. To select the best ones, go with your gut. If you have a question, find a book that promises to answer it. Have an interest? Follow that. By the way, you don't have to read only business books. In fact, Steve Sullivan from the Liberty Mutual Group offers this advice: "Successful managers read a lot and not just in their areas of expertise. They read about current events, history, culture, business, sports; they read fiction and nonfiction. Whatever the subject matter, reading gives them a broader perspective and allows them to place their company, department, and even their mission in a broader context." Take time to read something every day.

Q: Even if I did schedule time to read every day, I'd still get through only a few pages. How can I get enough reading time in to really benefit?

A. Great managers have interesting strategies for extrapolating information from a range of books. When you are reading nonfiction, jump to the segments that interest you most. Or use these books as a reference—find what you need when you need it.

Most managers know this instinctively but may feel guilty or like they're cheating if they don't read from beginning to end. Don't worry—just get the content you need and move on. I'm sure many of my readers take that approach with this book and others like it. That's why I divided the sections into self-contained units.

Martha Boudreau, an executive at Fleishman-Hillard International Communications, advocates book reading as a prerequisite to strong management. She has a rigorous and demanding work schedule that requires her to travel around the world and frequently work on weekends. She recommends that you skim through trade magazines—they usually contain excerpts from books. Then, if you find an author you like or helpful information, buy the book.

You might find a simple reading schedule helpful. For example, set aside fifteen or twenty minutes every day to read. If you commute to work, read on the train. If you have an early-morning cup of coffee, read as you drink. You can involve your employees, too. Here are a few ideas about how:

- Assign everyone a different chapter or two from a book. Then, at your weekly meetings, have one employee give a presentation about that chapter and have a brief discussion afterward. Your employees probably would be better off reading *The Seven Habits of Highly Effective People* and not, say, *War and Peace*, but the exercise will give everyone on your team valuable information *and* help stimulate their creativity and thought.
- Hold brown-bag lunches once a month where one member of the team reviews a book and leads a discussion about it. If possible, provide the lunch: this will encourage people to attend and help employees look forward to the meeting and not feel like it's a burden or extra work.
- Invite an author to speak to your group at a conference or even at a weekly meeting. Most authors I know are more than happy to give a thirty-minute presentation for free as a way of promoting their book, alerting you to their training abilities, and, above all, promoting their ideas.

Q. How about books on tape?

A. Books on tape are a great way to garner information on the go. But remember—you're multitasking. That means you won't retain as much of the information as if you were sitting down and reading, and you won't have the opportunity to take notes.

Q. Are white papers or blogs helpful for managers to read?

A. That can vary depending on the author. Some white papers may be articulate and useful; others might be a mere expression of the author's ego. As for blogs: if you find a professional whose blogs you enjoy, read them. You'll also grow as a manager by writing them. Writing forces you to think concepts through, organize your thoughts, and find ample support for every point. In some cases, you may find yourself researching information you thought you already knew. You may also get responses to your blog that force you to confront adversarial views or even reconsider your own.

If you're eager to call attention to your organization or ideas, you can also send your blogs to the opinion section of your local newspapers or, with a little more content and a highly fact-based approach, a trade magazine.

Q. Is it a good idea to attend conferences?

A. Yes, for many reasons. The most obvious is that you can learn a great deal from the sessions. Even more important, you'll speak with other professionals and get opportunities to exchange ideas, share books, and network. Just about every business association has a local and national chapter and many conferences and events—it can't hurt to join and, if you're really enthused, become an active participant.

You can also create a real opportunity for yourself by giving talks at the conferences. As with blogs, you'll have to double-check your thinking and, in academic venues, prepare ironclad defenses for what you know to be true. Even the process of drafting seminar proposals, which can entail a highly specific breakdown of content, will help you grow.

Q. How do I make sure a conference or training session is worthwhile before I sign up for it?

A. When looking for a good seminar, start by determining the outcome you want from the session. You could also choose a seminar that has little to do with your field and lets you take a break from your work life. This can prove surprisingly beneficial and rewarding and even enhance your abilities as a manager. For example, you may want to attend a seminar on biotechnology that will give you insights into innovations in other fields or learn a new skill, such as woodworking. One of my clients, at an airplane manufacturing plant, treated his staff to a square dancing session. They had a great time and indirectly learned new ways of working together.

Once you identify a seminar or series of classes you like, research the instructors, their approach to the material, and their credentials. You can get this information by googling them or calling the program director. Conversely, if you read a useful book or heard interviews with an expert on the radio, go to that person's website. Chances are he or she offers training or gives interesting talks you might enjoy.

Also, try to find professionals who have attended the session before. Make sure the instructor contextualizes the content, providing insights and ideas you can really use. For example, in one Myers Brigg session I took, the instructor continuously used examples of her children, her parents, and even her grandchildren—all of them alarmingly *cute*—even though the session was for mid-level managers. The information may have been true, but the participants would be hard-pressed to apply it to the workplace.

Be aware that you won't retain most of the information you garner from the session unless you immediately apply it. Think of it like taking a language class: Unless you practice and keep on practicing, you'll lose it fairly quickly. Unlike the subject matter in a language class, though, much of what you'll learn in management sessions will be less prescriptive and concrete. So, consider taking the session with a colleague, and follow up with discussions about how you applied the concepts once the seminar ended.

Chapter 2

MANAGING PEOPLE

Hiring and Recruiting: What Every Great Manager Should Know

- ■ I often think I've found the right employee, but once he or she is on board, I get some depressing, even alarming, surprises. Is there something wrong with my approach?
- ■ How important is a candidate's education?
- ■ What is the best way to find employees?
- ■ Should I be giving more information than the type of job, responsibilities, compensation, and so on? How do I market a position?
- ■ Are job announcements or other types of help-wanted signs or recruitment materials a form of marketing?
- ■ What kind of unexpected rewards can come from good job announcements?
- ■ In my marketing materials, should I focus on specific attributes of the job or make the description more general?
- ■ Is it okay to spin if you can't really find anything interesting about the job?
- ■ How involved should my employees be in the recruiting process?
- ■ At what point in the process should I arrange an interview?
- ■ What are some of the best strategies for interviewing candidates and getting the kind of information I really need to know?
- ■ Is there anything I should avoid saying in the job interview?
- ■ Once a new employee is on the job, how soon should I expect him or her to catch on?
- ■ Won't other employees be jealous of all the attention the new hire is getting?
- ■ How much time should I expect to devote to new employees?

Giving and Taking Feedback: The Endless Loop

- ■ What is the first step in providing feedback?
- ■ Should I determine the employees' objectives, or should they?

■ I have a hard time pinpointing my objectives. I have so many responsibilities and goals to reach, how can I narrow them down to five or six?

■ Our workplace is pretty volatile, constantly undergoing changes. So, what happens if we write objectives and they stop being relevant before the year's up?

■ Does it matter how I—or my employees—word the objectives?

■ In a lot of cases, I'm not sure there are any definable outcomes. So what should I do?

■ What if the projects are long-term? How can I establish objectives for something that goes on for years?

■ Some of my employees have tasks that take months to complete, so the outcomes aren't as recognizable as those achieved by employees with shorter-term projects. How do I let upper management know about the importance of their contributions if I don't have a lot of space to explain?

■ Does the order of information really make a difference in the review?

■ As a manager, much of what I do is long-term, process driven, and big picture. I can nail down my employees' outcomes, but how can I be specific about my own?

■ Do I need to provide feedback to my employees at times other than the annual review?

■ Which is better—spoken or written feedback?

■ Should I always give feedback in private?

■ Should I try to get feedback from my employees, or will it undermine my power?

■ What is the best way to provide negative feedback or give employees bad news?

■ Aren't there times when I should just come out and tell them that they dropped the ball?

■ What if I provide feedback several times and my employee *still* doesn't change?

Managing Difficult Employees

■ What is the best way to manage difficult employees?

■ How can I tell for sure whether an employee is passive-aggressive at work?

■ How do I deal with a passive-aggressive employee?

■ How can I address the issue of personal hygiene problems without embarrassing the employee it concerns?

- Once I am certain that the problem really does affect our work lives, what should I do?
- I've noticed that my employee has made rude sexual comments to a few of my female employees. Should I take action or let it go until they complain to me about the problem?
- How do I handle office gossips?
- Is it true that gossip is worse in all-female work environments?
- I'm a new manager, and I inherited an unmotivated workforce. What should I do?
- I find that employees settle into routines, stop paying attention to the requirements of the job, and then make ridiculous mistakes. What can I do about that?
- Are rewards programs effective?
- Are warnings and threats motivational?
- What are the best ways to motivate my employees?
- How should I approach employees who seem happy but don't seem to get much done?
- How do I handle an employee who is always negative, is constantly complaining, and disagrees with the other employees all the time?
- What should I do when an employee goes on a rant of complaints?
- What needs to happen if an employee gets angry in front of a customer?
- What should I do when an employee is angry with me?

Managing Disabled Employees

- I know it's not PC to feel this way, but I'm not sure how to deal with my disabled employees. Do other managers feel this way, too? What can I do to feel more comfortable?
- Three of my employees are deaf. How does this concept of eradicating my prejudices apply to them?
- What should I do to help integrate my disabled employees into the workplace?
- What should I do if I suspect that an employee has a mental illness?

Managing the Generation Gap

- I'm fifty-two years old and have a new crop of employees in their twenties whom I can't seem to keep motivated. Could I be experiencing a generation gap of some sort?
- I'm twenty-eight, and a guy who's about my dad's age is working for me. How should I handle him?

Managing the Gender Gap

- More than half my workforce is composed of women, and I feel that I should give them equal rights but I'm not even sure what that means. How should I proceed?

- If I'm too friendly or complimentary to my female employees, I'm afraid I'll be accused of harassment—but I don't want to be totally impersonal, either. Are there any guidelines about the right way to interact?

Cultural Diversity in the Workplace

- My employees come from a vast range of backgrounds. What is the best way to address some of the cultural differences at work?

- How can I get my employees to deal with their feelings of prejudice?

- My company is international, and I frequently interact with colleagues and clients halfway around the world. Should I expect them to recognize the cultural differences between us, or should I change my work style when working with them?

Managing Bosses

- I know it sounds crazy, but my boss is a bigger block to my department's progress than any of my employees are. What are some ways to manage her?

- My boss insists that every new assignment is top priority and assigns an excruciating deadline, so I'm constantly struggling to adjust my schedule and reassign my employees. What should I do?

- My boss is something of a bulldog—he has outbursts and can get really degrading. If he were an employee, I'd contact HR, keep a record of his behavior, and put him on probation. But because he's my boss, what can I do?

- My boss is unbelievably hands-off—she hides behind closed doors and appears only for meetings, and she's unable to give me any ideas or support (great evaluations, though). Should I just feel lucky she's not breathing down my neck?

Managing Clients

- My client keeps changing his mind about his project, which is costing us money and time and frustrating my employees. How should I handle this?

- What if I have to delay a project or charge more than I originally intended?

- What if I'm not sure exactly how much time I'll need?

- How should I approach a client who agrees to a project, thinks it's great, and is in a big hurry to get going—but then is never willing to actually start the work?

I've worked as a communications and management consultant since 1989, and a lot has changed since then. Typewriters are out; computers are in. Letters are out (or almost out), and emails are in. Employees once needed to show up at work, and now they can virtually commute.

In spite of all these changes, one thing remains the same: managers find their employees—with all their foibles, needs, demands, and potential—perplexing. This confusion makes sense. Where do you learn how to manage *people?* What guidelines can you follow when you have employees with poor, even distracting tics and traits, such as bad personal hygiene? How do you handle an embarrassingly rude employee in a meeting you're facilitating with clients? You may find yourself in many unlikely scenarios as a manager, and you should be prepared.

Hiring and Recruiting: What Every Great Manager Should Know

The best way to manage employees is to find employees who are great. Good managers rely on an applicant's past job requirements, but great managers search for applicants who will contribute to the overall environment so their team can be even stronger. Finding those employees can be an art, but mostly it's a strategy and, of course, a science.

Q. I often think I've found the right employee, but once he or she is on board, I get some depressing, even alarming, surprises. Is there something wrong with my approach?

A. Possibly. When looking for employees, you need to be thoughtful and systematic. Your first step should be to closely examine your expectations of the new employee. Take a *fresh* look—don't rely on past expectations—and, above all, don't try to find an exact duplicate of the employee you're replacing. Then, when meeting with the candidate, consider these questions:

- *How well does that person's work style fit with the group?* You can get insights into this intangible question right from the start. Consider where the applicant was previously employed: If it's a fast-paced, edgy organization and so is yours, the applicant might fit right in. If it's a large organization where employees get intense oversight, and you expect self-reliance, hiring this person might not work. Of course, the employee may have left one job hoping for a profoundly different work experience in the next—if so, get clear answers about the candidate's expectations.
- *How much experience should the candidate have?* The answer may seem evident—the more the better. But that's not necessarily so. Candidates who have worked in a particular position for a long time may be set in their ways, and teaching them your approach may be difficult. For example, over the years, I've hired numerous writers for my business. The writers with the most experience, who have been in the corporate world the longest, have the worst problems with clichés, boring language, troubled structure—all typical problems in corporate communications. But employees with less experience are often more open to feedback and more willing to change.
- *How does that person's experience fit with your company's requirements?* Of course, you want employees who are experts in your field. But complementary experience may reign over direct experience, depending on the qualifications you want. Say you're hiring a project manager—the right person may not be familiar with your industry, but if the applicant has experience managing complex and intense projects, he or she could bring a lot to the position.
- *How long has the candidate remained in one job?* In this era of

changeable jobs, candidates often are on the lookout for better money or experience. In an interview, of course, they'll vehemently insist that this isn't the case, but check their résumés carefully: if they have a history of remaining in any position for only a year, two at most, chances are they won't last with you, either.

Of course, some firms think of the transitory nature as a plus. One of my clients, an international consulting firm, assumes its employees will have a short, happy tenure; then they'll move on and call from their next job to request consulting services. More likely, though, you'll want to find employees whom you can train, mentor, and otherwise invest in, and they, in turn, will contribute for the long term.

Q. How important is a candidate's education?

A. The candidate's education may be overrated. I say "may" because that depends on the position you're trying to fill; if you are hiring nuclear physicists or surgeons, obviously they must have multiple degrees. If you're hiring an attorney, a law degree is essential.

But must that degree come from an Ivy League school? It's always nice to know your employees graduated from Yale—but that doesn't mean they'll be excellent performers. In fact, a friend of mine, an attorney who actually did go to Yale, confided that she was a much better, and more inspired, student than attorney. And she was amazed that her colleagues, who attended far lesser schools, actually excelled in their positions. Similarly, I once had a dean who had gotten his doctorate from Oxford. Quite clearly, the search committee had been blinded by the name of the school on his degree—his tenure was hardly a success.

Granted, these examples are anecdotal. My point is simply that the people, and what they derived from the education, matter more than the name on their degrees.

Q. What is the best way to find employees?

A. You can go to any number of places to search for new hires:

- **Current employees and friends.** This option seems to be the most popular one. Most managers swear by it, and most of the how-to articles online and elsewhere recommend it first. I agree—your employees know what the job requires and can identify people who will participate on the terms you need.

  However, there are potential hazards to this strategy. If your employee effusively recommends a friend or colleague but you decide on another candidate, he or she may be resentful and biased against the newcomer. Or, if an employee recommends someone who doesn't work out, unnecessary friction between you and the employee could result. Finally, the new employee might have unrealistic expectations of the workplace thanks to your employee's experience—something especially hazardous in a small firm.

- **Hiring an employment or executive search firm.** These firms vary in their approach to finding people—some simply collect résumés, whereas others build relationships with candidates, carefully screening each one to find the right person for a job.

- **Placing newspaper ads or postings online.** Whether you should place an ad in a print publication or online posting is up to you. Both can work reasonably well and will bring interest to the job. Both target specific audiences. For example, online postings through associations or the blog community or ads in a trade magazine can reach thousands of people who are already in the business. In these venues you must vie for the candidate's attention, creating the most interesting and alluring (and honest) description of the position possible.

In spite of these similarities, online and print ads are not the same. Consider the audiences they attract: most people over fifty years old choose hard-copy newspapers as a primary news source, while only 36 percent under age fifty do so. An over-whelming majority of professionals regardless of age use the web, and CEOs and executives consider the Internet their main source of business news.

However, before you decide how to advertise open positions, think about your business, the job, and the candidate you want. If your business is in a small town and there is a bank of suitable local talent, put an ad in the local newspaper: the employee you want may see it and, if not, plenty of people who know that person will tell him or her about it. But if you're in technology and looking for an innovative developer, online venues are your most logical option.

- **Hiring fairs, particularly on campuses.** These events work well if you work for a company that can afford a booth and has many openings to promote. But your booth must be excep-tional: you are no longer *announcing* a position; you're *marketing* one. Make no mistake: the competition is strong and real for the upper tier of talent. If you give anything less than 100 percent effort, targeted strategy will lead to failure.

Q. Should I be giving more information than the type of job, responsibilities, compensation, and so on? How do I market a position?

A. Quite possibly, you are missing something. You need to find ways to make your open position seem worth the candidates' time, inter-ests, and, of course, years of their lives. In essence, you're selling the position and must use sound marketing strategies.

One place to start is to find a tagline that will attract the talent you want. This phrase would be separate from your company's tagline and belongs only in your hiring materials. Beware of clichés and make sure the tagline speaks directly to the job. For example, plenty of companies use phrases such as "The future begins here"—concepts that are so obvious, they're meaningless. Find something that both accurately expresses the job and intrigues people:

- "Good living begins here" (Adams Nursery)
- "Where a job becomes an experience"
- "The right career move in a perfect location" (Chambers Real Estate Associates)

Then put the tagline on your career brochures, the "career" section of your website, and any other place potential applicants might look. Don't deviate from the style of your organization, but keep the tagline crisp, clear, and original.

If you are presenting at a job fair, you'll need to bring giveaways. Everyone loves them and, with the right product, candidates will flock to your table. Once they arrive, you or your representative can talk to them about the job. The only caveat is to make sure your prospect will actually use the giveaway and that it naturally relates to the job. So, for example, if you work in an engineering firm, give away rulers with your firm's name, URL, and phone number emblazoned on them. Whatever you do, do *not* give them a pen (everyone gives pens and most people lose them), a squeeze ball (why equate your company with stress?), or a beach ball (who uses beach balls on a job search and, besides, what does a beach ball have to do with your organization anyway?).

Most important, remember when marketing a position to make sure your efforts are consistent with your firm's other marketing and advertising messages. So, if your firm's brand is built around the idea of quality and integrity, don't try to sell the job as cool and trendy. If you have a snappy image and pool tables and beverage machines in your conference rooms, don't let the language create a tired, old-fashioned impression.

Q. Are job announcements or other types of help-wanted signs or recruitment materials a form of marketing?

A. Absolutely—and much more than that. In fact, managers consistently underestimate the power of job announcements and settle for descriptions that are mind-numbingly boring. They approach them as a simple list of roles, responsibilities, and rewards and the criteria necessary to get them—more of a policy document than anything else.

In reality, job announcements are of irreplaceable value. But—and this point is critical—you cannot tap that power unless you get personally involved in crafting the message. Even if you delegate this responsibility, review the copy carefully. If you use a template, update it every time you need to fill a position. You'll also find that a well-thought-out job announcement brings in unexpected rewards.

Q. What kind of unexpected rewards can come from good job announcements?

A. It's no secret that the exodus of baby boomers continues to take prized employees out of the workforce; in these cases, job announcements written by the experienced professionals leaving the positions can double as knowledge management tools—descriptions of the jobs that form the building blocks of your organization written by the people who know them best.

Whether your job announcements are up to this task is debatable; if you've been using a template that's been in your department for years, you need to revise incorrect and outdated information. Also, content problems infiltrate most business writing; in fact, more than half of the thousands of documents my employees have reviewed over the years contain inaccuracies no one—neither writer nor reviewer—managed to catch. Even if your job announcement is relatively current, look for these sorts of mistakes.

Part of this process will mean fine-tuning your language and replacing jargon and problem grammar with clearer alternatives. This is an issue not of style but of content. Poor wording frequently obscures meaning and renders the announcement (or any other document, for that matter) useless. For example, one line from a federal job announcement I reviewed a few years back read as follows: *This is a permanent, career-conditional appointment.* This could mean that the appointment is permanently conditional and offers no security or that it is permanent only under certain circumstances.

By the way, you can turn the task of drafting a job announcement and related materials into a morale-boosting opportunity for your staff. Have them write a list of what they most like about working for your company. For example, if you're based in New York City, they might like the location. If you're working for a conservation group, they may appreciate the chance to spend time in a forest. This exercise alone can reinforce what your employees like about the job and help them think in positive terms about their work—real, honest terms that resonate with them and can resonate with job seekers, too.

Q. In my marketing materials, should I focus on specific attributes of the job or make the description more general?

A. In general, your marketing material should focus on the attributes that will interest your primary candidate most. For example, if you're recruiting on a college campus, your prospects are obviously educated and in their twenties. They want something different, something more than the security and stability of a good job—although they want that, too. Here are a few things you'll want to convey:

1. **A position with integrity.** At a recent conference, I was giving a talk about strategies for positioning jobs. I mentioned that the announcements should play up the positive aspects of the job. A participant asked how this was possible when some have no positive attributes, and other people seconded the sentiment. So be sure you, as a manager, and the employee drafting the job description (not to mention your entire workforce) recognize the true value of the job.

   In his book *Working,* Chicago writer Studs Terkel provides a clue about how to find this value. He interviewed everyone from CEOs to bathroom attendants, and what he uncovered was that every employee—the truly good ones, anyway—found something to love about their jobs, something to take pride in, some aspect of the job where they could be best. The measure of their success ultimately was not financial but through ownership of a job well done.

   Most likely, every position you advertise has an intrinsic value, something you cannot do without. Mail clerks, for example, ensure the flow of information from one office to the next; customer service representatives answer questions, calm customers, and solve problems that could cost your organization untold amounts of goodwill and dollars. Each marketing message should reflect the integrity of the specific job it's advertising as precisely as possible.

2. **Service to the community and the world.** Making a living and raising a family are values that most candidates embrace. But

they want something else, too—to better the world around them. Your messages can reflect this in the simplest of terms. For example, if you are a manager in a bank, you can cite your company's mission in a sentence like this: "You will join a team of banking professionals intent on helping customers better manage their money." Or you can point to an outcome, such as this ad for a sales position: "Sell the most affordable and highest-quality packages to the consumers who most deserve them." You can also mention any charitable organizations your company serves.

3. **Dynamic responsibilities.** Depending on your firm, the position, and its level, you can offer challenges that intrigue the candidate. Exposing these advantages requires that you focus on the readers' interests and perceptions of themselves. Notice that *career* is more professional and rewarding than *job*, for example. Bureaucratic headers such as "Qualification Requirements" can be more personal in a Q&A format such as "What background do I need for this position?" More creative approaches are helpful, too, such as a "Checklist of Qualifications" or, for a younger, more targeted candidate, "Do you have what it takes?"

Q. Is it okay to spin if you can't really find anything interesting about the job?

A. No—it's never right to lie or even exaggerate. In essence, you're making a promise in a job announcement that you need to keep. Conversely, in an effort to be forthright, many managers unintentionally play down the value of the job or fail to mention aspects of their company that the job seeker is sure to like. Even worse, they use dry language that gives the candidate the impression that it's a boring, staid environment.

What does all this mean? You must approach the hiring initiative as a publicist—you are selling a position, and your targets are the best possible candidates for the job. But it's *essential* that you love and believe in your product. If you're not sure, as we mentioned earlier, go back to the employees and ask what they love and value about the job. Then the virtues will naturally surface.

In addition, look and listen for the positive language and ideas that bubble up around you. Perhaps you hear your employees say things like, "We are really hardworking." Or perhaps you overhear someone say that you have more experts on staff than your competitors do. Maybe you consistently say things like, "I always knew we'd come up with another great solution!" Capture this language and embed it in your job descriptions.

Q. How involved should my employees be in the recruiting process?

A. You definitely should involve employees in recruiting, but be aware of when and why you're doing it. In writing the job announcement, get their input *before* you or your employee actually writes the copy. As we discussed, it's important to learn what your employees value about the organization and, for that matter, what the position you're hoping to fill really has to offer. Also, it can be helpful to get insights into the skills, particularly soft skills such as writing, the applicant needs for the job from people doing similar work. Avoid asking for feedback once you've finished the copy, however: chances are you'll only get subjective and not-very-useful comments.

The interview is a different matter. You do want to engage the employees in the interview process—not all the employees, of course, but a select group. Whom you invite depends on their position. Pick employees likely to lead projects, work with the candidate, or rely on the candidate. Here's why: your employees can give you additional insights into the candidate and offset any bias you may bring to the interview. For example, you may have attended the same college as the candidate and feel drawn to him or her, although this particular candidate may not be as strong as other candidates. Your employees can help you see applicants with clarity.

In addition, you need to see the chemistry between your employees and the candidate. Of course, likability isn't the only reason for hiring someone, but as we discussed, you are changing the environment with every new employee who enters your department. You want that change to be positive. Finally, you want to win your employees' support of the choice so that they immediately accept the candidate once he or she becomes an employee.

Q. At what point in the process should I arrange an interview?

A. Obviously, you'll need to look through the applications and decide which ones interest you. From there, consider conducting a telephone interview before actually bringing the person in; it takes less time, so if you don't like the candidate, you won't waste much of your day. If the candidate does well during the phone interview, invite him or her in for a face-to-face meeting.

Depending on the situation, good managers may have one or two employees interview the candidates to narrow down the choices to the top two or three; only then does the manager participate. Great managers do this, too, but they also do something else: plan for the interview before even the telephone interview.

As part of your planning process, draft a list of outcomes you want the employee to achieve once he or she takes the job, and compare them to the outcomes the candidate achieved in previous positions. An easy example is a sales representative. Did the candidate meet his or her quotas? Exceed them? And was he or she able to maintain this momentum for numerous years? You'll need to find out.

Then, develop a list of questions for the candidate based on your criteria. Most managers have a hard time at this stage—they tend to create a fantasy employee and see how the real candidates measure up, or they look at the best employee they've ever seen and base the criteria on him or her. Instead, determine your criteria based on the realities of the job.

You can take two other steps: look into the reasons why other new hires at your company have failed at their jobs, and conduct a thorough background check. The HR Chally Group, a consulting company, offers good advice on its website, www.chally.com: "Research consistently shows that people fail in a job due to factors different from the criteria used to select them." Is your business a perfect setup for failure? Or were the conditions that led to their failures unavoidable, no matter who was involved? A careful background check means looking into police records, talking to references, and finding evidence that what the applicant says is true.

Finally, as unscientific as it is, trust your gut. If you really like someone whose qualifications aren't quite up to snuff, don't automatically rule out that person. And if you find a candidate who's perfect on paper, but with whom you just don't think you click, don't ignore your intuition. Bring in others to help you make the decision if you need to, but always trust your gut.

Q. What are some of the best strategies for interviewing candidates and getting the kind of information I really need to know?

A. Interviews can be awkward because they have an artificial quality: you and the candidate are set on making an impression while simultaneously sizing each other up. It's almost like a date. In many cases, the candidate has more experience with the interview process than you do, especially if he or she has had coaching from school advisors, outplacement firm professionals, or trial and error. This means the candidate may be able to drive the discussion and steal valuable learning time from you.

Be sure to bring your notes to the session and stick to them. Don't let the conversation get derailed with talk about sports teams or personal anecdotes from your or the candidate's past. However, you don't want to entirely miss out on personal interactions either. If the talk turns to banter, let it proceed for just a few minutes, and then return to your list.

Although you want to take control of the interview and get across all the information you need to, be sure to let the candidate talk, too: in fact, 75 percent or so of the interview time, the candidate should be talking. Your mission, of course, is to learn who the candidate really is—which means stripping away the polite veneer and getting down to business.

As you interview, watch those leading questions. For example, if you say something like, "Why do you enjoy traveling for work?" prospective employees will immediately explain why they enjoy it. What you really want to know is whether they're willing to travel, have experience doing it, and can feel comfortable in hotel rooms night after night. Ask specific questions to get the details you need.

Similarly, avoid giving away answers. For example, if you said, "Does $50,000 a year and one week paid vacation seem fair to you?" you're giving away the job offer. Most candidates would nod their heads and say, "Yes, $50,000 was what I was hoping for," even if they were willing to work for $40,000. Instead, ask what salary range they have in mind.

Q. Is there anything I should avoid saying in the job interview?

A. Mike Poskey, vice president of ZERORISK HR, Inc., a Dallas-based human resources risk management firm, states that "it's important for interviewers to be familiar with topics that aren't permissible as interview questions . . . asking the wrong interview questions or making improper inquiries can lead to discrimination or wrongful-discharge lawsuits, and these suits can be won or lost based on statements made during the interview process."

Among the questions that Poskey cautions managers to avoid are the following:

- Don't ask a female candidate about her family or her family plans. It can reappear as proof of sexual discrimination later.
- Don't ask older candidates—or any candidate, for that matter—their age or if they are willing to work for younger bosses.
- Avoid descriptions such as *permanent, career opportunity,* or *long-term.* Poskey says they suggest an employment contract.
- Avoid promissory language about job security, including saying things like, "If you do a good job, we'll let you stay on," or "If you work hard and make your goals, we'll promote you." If the employee does a great job but gets laid off anyway because of a layoff, she can claim breach of contract.

Of course, you should also familiarize yourself with the laws in your state and make sure you are up-to-date on the laws that govern business conduct—you could even run your list of questions by the company's attorney just to be sure.

Q. Once a new employee is on the job, how soon should I expect him or her to catch on?

A. How soon a new hire is able to function independently depends on your team, the employee, and the complexity of the job. As a manager, though, you can help employees ease into the transition in a number of ways. One is to establish a time frame for each of their new tasks. Be sure to provide a list of steps and resources that will help. You can also establish a mentoring program where you, another manager, or another employee mentors the new hires. This can entail anything from showing them around the office to letting them shadow you for a period of time.

This arrangement can provide numerous benefits. Employees who serve as mentors can build their leadership skills, test their own knowledge base, and contribute to the company. And, of course, they have the satisfaction of making the transition better for someone else. However, make sure you choose mentors who can juggle the responsibility with their regular workload.

Q. Won't other employees be jealous of all the attention the new hire is getting?

A. That's an interesting question and one I discussed with Nancy Mills, executive director of the AFL-CIO Working for America Institute. According to Mills, one important aspect of a healthy work environment is that employees get treated fairly and equally. That's not to say that everyone makes the same amount of money or gets promoted at the same time, but they should have equal opportunities to do so. Make sure you offer the same opportunity to all new hires. Do they all have access to new training or other tools that help them excel? Are these tools available to all your employees as well? There will be no occasion for jealousy in your office if everyone is given equal opportunity to succeed.

Q. How much time should I expect to devote to new employees?

A. Again, that depends on your organization. If it's small, you may not have a choice—you need to spend as much time as is necessary to get them on their feet. If it's large, you may be able to easily delegate that responsibility to someone else. Regardless, don't pitch new employees into the waters and expect them to swim. Show them your in-house manuals and arrange an orientation for them. Also, give them a project list for the next few weeks, incrementally adding on more difficult or complex tasks. At each point, give them the freedom to excel in one area before moving on. If the employees want more responsibility, all the better—just make sure they can handle it before giving them something incredibly important or time-sensitive.

Giving and Taking Feedback: The Endless Loop

Feedback serves as the backbone of a strong department. It gives employees a context for their responsibilities so they know whether, and how, their efforts are paying off. But feedback does more than that: it motivates employees, sets a direction for achieving in the future, influences the department's culture, and establishes a dynamic between employees. Naturally, every employee wants positive feedback—they want to know they are appreciated and valued.

Knowing this, many managers make the serious mistake of focusing on positive points, often irrespective of the employee's performance. This feel-good approach undermines the value of the feedback, demoralizes employees who know they are unable to trust it, and ultimately interferes with the department's well-being. Even managers who know this find giving honest, well-balanced feedback difficult if not grueling, so they reserve the negative comments for dire situations when it's often too late.

Q. What is the first step in providing feedback?

A. The first step of feedback occurs well before you start giving it—when your employees write their objectives. In fact, most managers pay too little attention to objectives, although, when used correctly, they can serve a useful role in supporting your management efforts. They can point your department, and individual employees, in specific directions and help you measure their failures and successes.

Q. Should I determine the employees' objectives, or should they?

A. Ideally your employees should determine their own objectives, based on previous feedback, the department's or company's missions, and their professional aspirations. Then, together, review these objectives and provide feedback. At times, you will also need to identify their contributions; the employees simply may not recognize them although they repeat the tasks daily. This can be a great motivator.

For example, the support staff at a manufacturing company had to ensure that all relevant information, including last-minute changes, was inserted in their computer system so the 500-plus employees received their paychecks on time. They also had to address ongoing questions from the employees about, for example, how to make changes using the often-confusing forms, how to find information online, and when people would receive additional compensation such as pay increases and bonuses.

Their objectives were clear: ensure that employees get paid on time and provide accurate responses to inquiries within twenty-four hours. But the staff didn't identify these tasks as being valuable—it was simply what they did. When the manager pointed this out and helped them build objectives around their responsibilities, they had a renewed sense of purpose. Then they added new, more challenging objectives that would benefit the organization and fuel their growth.

Make sure they also incorporate objectives that target individual performance issues. For example, most managers have employees who chronically show up late for work and meetings, miss deadlines, and start projects when they should be finishing them. Then they try to compensate by staying late after work and frantically working on weekends.

This is more than a personal work style: it disrupts your employees' ability to work as a team and have a trusting and meaningful work relationship with each other. If the manager doesn't address this issue, or address it in a meaningful way, the team will feel undercut—as they should.

Finally, never give one employee inordinate goals or those that differ in scope or duration from other employees' goals. If one employee has two months to learn how to use the software, then others must also get a full two months.

Here are a few other requirements for objectives:

- Make the objectives specific to certain projects. Let's say you have a sales team who must learn to incorporate online resources into their sales strategies. Rather than set a general objective of using the online strategies, be specific. What product or sales initiative should they begin with? At what point—or points—in the sales cycle should they begin? Give them explicit, clearly defined goals to hit to be sure they are progressing appropriately.
- Target a concrete or otherwise definable outcome. You don't want employees to be floating in space, hoping to do good work: you want them to target *evidence* of that good work. For example, if you manage a customer service center, what evidence do you have that your employees are succeeding? Did they receive fewer repeat calls from confused customers than they did the previous year? Did they consistently walk

If you are discussing:	Your outcome would look like this:
Cycle time	I will cut the time necessary to develop a product from eight weeks to three.
Percent	My goal is to cut costs in the first phase of the project by 25%.
Dollars	I plan to stay within budget although the scope of our project is broader.
Employee time	My team will complete the analysis in three months, freeing employees to begin the new initiative in early September.
Feedback	At least 90% of the reviews I give will be excellent.
Steps	I should complete the project in three stages, not five.

customers through certain steps that helped them reach clear and specific goals? Did they get high marks from a survey?

Here are a few more examples:
- Directly affect someone or something. The person or thing affected could be a system, department, client, or fellow employee—just find ways to connect your employees' actions to a higher goal, something with deeper values. Make sure they provide ample, objective evidence of achieving this.
- Relate to an aspect of your company's mission or values. This mission may be overt, such as providing stellar customer care, or built into the culture of your organization. Say your company prides itself on being innovative—maybe a little edgy. No one actually *says* that, but the edginess, that new way of doing things, is integral to everything from the organizational design of your company to the value of your services. So, it makes sense that your employees will have, as an objective, a

new and better way of accomplishing certain tasks.

- Have a specific end. You need to determine time frames for your objectives. Let's say the employees are launching a new website, providing information about how citizens can create a greener environment. At what point should that website be complete? In the first quarter of the year? How many visitors should they try to attract? How much time should each visitor spend on the site? These are measurable marks of success.

Q. I have a hard time pinpointing my objectives. I have so many responsibilities and goals to reach, how can I narrow them down to five or six?

A. Plenty of managers have that problem. If you're unsure about which objectives to target—or find the process of determining them slow or arduous—take the following steps:

Step 1: *Write every objective you can imagine for the upcoming year.* If you're using a formal appraisal system and have numerous performance elements, write as many objectives as possible for each. Write quickly: don't monitor your statements or try to fine-tune the language. And, above all, don't worry about repeating objectives, adding too many, or writing the wrong ones. This is a brain dump.

Step 2: *Review and streamline the objectives.* Weed out low-priority objectives and combine overlapping ones. For example, you may want your department to answer fewer questions from customers—not because your employees aren't responsive, but because your processes should be clear without the customers having to ask questions. If another objective states that your department should quicken the customer service process, combine the two objectives. By addressing fewer questions, the customer service process will naturally speed up.

Step 3: *Organize the remaining statements according to order of importance.* Try to base your priorities not on the amount of time reaching an objective takes but on the value of the outcome. If you're in research, for example, one objective may be to secure proper funding—a task that can take months to achieve. You may also be having trouble getting through one stage of the testing process. If you fail, the repercussions could be deadly for the project at worst and demoralizing for your employees no matter what. Although this particular stage of the process takes a month, maybe less, it deserves priority status.

Similarly, you may need to publish your findings in trade or academic publications. Once you write the article, sending it to editors may take thirty minutes. But the importance of getting the articles published is critical: it brings your team credibility and underscores the value of your work to potential funders. In many cases, your findings may also better the lives of others—but only if you get the word out.

Step 4: *Cut extra words and refine the language in other ways, if necessary.* This will help you create the smooth, easy language that's critical to strong objectives.

Q. Our workplace is pretty volatile, constantly undergoing changes. So, what happens if we write objectives and they stop being relevant before the year's up?

A. Remember—the objectives should not be a contract etched in cement for all time. Instead, they should be flexible depending on shifting company requirements and your employees' development. This means you should review the objectives at least every quarter. Sit down and discuss your employees' progress. Did they reach their goals? Did they need to leave one set of objectives and take on new, even more time-consuming ones midyear? Adapt the objectives, taking stock of your employees' progress at that point. Individuals' objectives should change with their additional roles and responsibilities, whether it's time for their formal review or not.

Q. Does it matter how I—or my employees—word the objectives?

A. Yes. And the principles of wording objectives also apply to the feedback you give employees, whether talking to them in one-on-one meetings or writing in-depth evaluations. To start, it's crucial that you use objective words that create clear and unambiguous goals. Notice the difference between these objective and subjective statements:

Subjective: You need to work harder.
Objective: You need to increase the number of client reports from three a year to ten a year.

As you may notice, objective language is actionable. You can't prove that your employees need to work harder, nor can you determine when they are, if there are not measurable signs of it. Besides, do you really care how hard they're working? Aren't you more concerned with the outcomes of their actions? Objective language allows that to happen.

Objective language, by the way, is *critical* when giving negative feedback to employees. Objective language takes the emotion out of your statement. Saying that your employee needs to work harder implies that he or she doesn't work hard or, in short, is lazy. This can work against you in numerous ways. The employee will feel insulted rather than motivated. You can lose your standing as a leader and become, instead, an adversary. Besides, subjective comments don't hold up in an EEO situation; in fact, they will work against you.

Here are some other examples of the difference between subjective and objective language:

Subjective	Objective
Large improvement	25 percent more efficient
Better	Cut questions due to misunderstandings in half
More	From eighteen to twenty
Consistent	The fifth of every month
Well-done	Receive approval the first time
Frequent	Weekly
Difficult	Two malfunctions

Another important and often overlooked aspect of strong objectives is the active voice. You need to ensure that your sentences have a clear actor/action/object relationship. For example, "I will host a conference for our clients" is a much clearer sentence than "A conference will be hosted for our clients."

The active voice spares you the problem of ambiguity and helps you cut unnecessary words, which can cloud meaning. If you're using a form with space limits, cutting unnecessary words will be critical.

Finally, you need to be as concise as possible. Here are some ways to achieve that—you'll find more in Chapter Four:

• Omit qualifiers such as *very* and *really*, which take up extra space but bring little value.

- Avoid prepositional phrases such as "in the event that . . ." or "in order to . . ." Replace them with one-word alternatives such as *if* or *to*.
- Cut unnecessary words, as in this example: "I will reach my department's goals."
- Avoid redundant language—such as, "I will provide excellent customer service to our customers." Who else could receive it?

Q. In a lot of cases, I'm not sure there are any definable outcomes. So what should I do?

A. Trust me—if you're in an organization with goals, cycle time issues, client expectations, deadlines, and profits, you have outcomes. Let's start with one basic reality: everything that occurs within an organization has a price tag attached to it. Let's look at a sales initiative. You may think the outcome is easy: how many new clients you brought in and how much that amounted to in terms of profits. But, actually, a lot more is involved than that. Most likely, your salesperson has a commission and base pay. So, here's the breakdown of quantifiable outcomes:

- Amount of time, per hour, salesperson must spend on the deal
- Amount of profits lost or gained before the customer starts the first payment
- Cost of resources, presentations, hotel bills, car mileage, and so on that the salesperson used to close the deal
- Duration of time and resulting profits from the client over months and years versus the expense of getting and keeping them

Here are a few other examples:

Task	Outcome
Customer support employees who help customers who are confused about their bills	Cycle time for getting the payments in; cost of employee time per hour taking repeated calls from frustrated customers; cost of employee time for follow-up calls
Administrative support person	Hours the administrative support person saved colleagues in getting material, routing messages, and so on in terms of the costs per employee per hour; expenses he or she saved within the department by finding better and less costly alternatives to usual practices
Manager of manufacturing plant	Employees' productivity; costs saved for accidents in the warehouse in terms of medical expenses, overall productivity, and replacement costs; quality of product in terms of recalls or parts replacements
Trainer	Time, in terms of employee hours, for employee to learn and apply skill; amount of time and resulting money the skill generated or saved the company

So, basically, you can always find measurable outcomes—it's just a matter of looking.

Q. What if the projects are long-term? How can I establish objectives for something that goes on for years?

A. You know the old expression about the best way to eat an elephant—one bite at a time. Every long-term project consists of small steps that you must complete before moving on to the next one. So, focus on those steps when determining your objectives.

I recently had a client with a strong research and development department. Most of the employees were engineers, all driven to find new and better ways of developing defense aircraft. However, because the majority of their R&D clients were military organizations, they never applied any of their findings no matter how remarkable—they developed the new aircraft only to defend against attacks that never occurred. Then they went on to develop new and better alternatives, staying one step ahead of the combat universe.

Many of the managers felt they had no outcomes to report. But their effort clearly wasn't in vain, nor did they squander taxpayer dollars. They were looking at their outcomes from a larger scale than necessary. Instead, they needed to narrow down their objectives. For example, one objective could have been the success rate of their tests and the associated costs of success or failure. Another could have been the future projects their breakthroughs and successes created.

Q. Some of my employees have tasks that take months to complete, so the outcomes aren't as recognizable as those achieved by employees with shorter-term projects. How do I let upper management know about the importance of their contributions if I don't have a lot of space to explain?

A. Brevity can be a problem with assessment tools, but there is an effective solution. However, it's important to remember that the real value of a review process is not to record how well an employee performed, although that *is* important. Instead, the assessment tools give you an opportunity to speak with your employees, check on their progress, guide them in productive directions, and address—or, even better, eliminate—roadblocks.

As for how you word those end-of-year reviews, this strategy works well for everything from one-line to ten-page reviews and can apply equally well when you're evaluating your own performance.

Essentially, break down each statement that you'd like to make, regardless of length, into three components: task, action, and outcome. So, for example, you might say the following:

Task	Action	Outcome
• Produced four systems reports, with our team and the clients' representatives, which passed review the first time, expediting the process by three weeks • Responded to employee questions electronically and by phone within twenty-four hours, so all weekly deadlines were met 100 percent of the time throughout the year		

Of course, you can reorder the statement so that it looks like this:

Task	Outcome	Action
• Quickened the development process by 25 percent by cutting the number of inquires in half and avoiding redundancies at all times • Cut customer questions from twenty a month to one or two by providing accessible information		

Or you could cut to the chase and simply write what you did and why it mattered:

Task	Outcome
• Dropped the number of adjustments in half • Kept production level steady and avoided the need to hire contractors	

Putting the employee's accomplishments into this kind of bare-bones, easy-to-comprehend language will make it clear to anyone who reads the review that this employee has been performing well in his or her job. This wording should make your employee's accomplishments clear to anyone who reads it.

Q. Does the order of information really make a difference in the review?

A. The order can help accentuate the most significant accomplishment in the statement. As a general rule, people pay the least attention to whatever is in the middle of a statement and the greatest attention to what comes first. So, place the most important, and impressive, information first. For example, one of my client's employees spent considerable time drafting reports but completed only two a year. The other employees, on average, completed eight. But this employee was different: he was smarter, more experienced, and more adept at compiling reports and so was delegated the more complex, lengthy, and demanding ones to write. So my client, in reviewing this employee, wrote: "Produced two 300-page reports with inputs from stakeholders in all core areas in 20 percent less time than previous efforts."

Notice how the "300-page" comes at the beginning of the sentence to immediately demonstrate the enormity of this effort. By providing these details, the manager was able to demonstrate the importance of his employee's task. He couldn't discuss the ultimate outcomes of the reports—they wouldn't be available for months—but the manager did note that the employee expedited the process of getting results by working closely with stakeholders and cutting down the expense associated with his time by 20 percent.

Q. As a manager, much of what I do is long-term, process driven, and big picture. I can nail down my employees' outcomes, but how can I be specific about my own?

A. This is an easy one. As a manager, you are responsible for your team's performance. Therefore, your objectives are the team's objectives—their success (or failure) depends on you. Say you wanted to lead your team to greater profitability, better customer service, or a higher production rate. Did you succeed? These goals should be easy to quantify and explain.

Q. Do I need to provide feedback to my employees at times other than the annual review?

A. Absolutely. In fact, feedback should be a regular part of your management duties. Be careful, though—most managers wait until trouble occurs to provide feedback, and at that point, it may be too late to do any good. You don't have to provide feedback in a formal setting, either. Ellen Tunstall, a former senior executive for the federal government, has managed hundreds of employees over the years. She says, "A good way to check in with employees and learn more about their work style is to walk through the office and observe what they're doing." It's important that you watch and listen quietly and with respect. Remember: you aren't spying on them; you're observing, openly and without unnecessary judgment.

Tunstall also recommends that you have regular and direct interactions. "Start a conversation with them whenever the opportunity hits," she says. "Ask what they do best, what pushes them most . . . Make sure this exchange is ongoing. You should also hold formal meetings with your employees at least once a quarter. At this point, check in, see how they're doing, review their objectives, check their plans, and reassess, with them, the direction they're taking."

Q. Which is better—spoken or written feedback?

A. Generally, use both. Spoken feedback is useful because you can interact with the employee, address questions, and clear up any miscommunications before they fester and become painful for everyone. Besides, communicating an exact tone is easier when you're speaking; writing tends to sound more formal and, in the reader's mind, more serious or negative than speech. If you're praising the employee in passing or giving feedback about a small point that the employee needs to correct, the spoken word can stand on its own.

But you should also write the feedback for several reasons. First, people tend to remember more of what they read than what they hear because they have a visual imprint, hear the words in their inner ear, and spend more time with the message. Also, they can always reread a written review.

Equally important, the written document can underscore important points or agreements that resulted from your discussion. In this sense, you are creating a game plan, a contract, that both of you agree on. Say you had a disagreement with an employee over a behavior issue. By the end of the discussion you reach an accord— the employee agrees to adopt certain new behaviors, and you agree to make provisions that will enable that to occur. These words may make everyone feel good, but ultimately that's all they are—words.

Once you or your employee writes them down, though, you have created an agreement and cemented the deal.

This leads to yet another reason for you to provide written feedback—it will serve as a paper trail should problems arise. This can be helpful if you need to fire the employee, recommend corrective action, turn him or her down for a raise or promotion, or even defend yourself against accusations.

Finally, whether you communicate through writing or speaking also depends on your and your employee's personal styles. If your employee is an introvert, for example, he or she may not know how to respond to spoken feedback. The employee will need to process the information, test it, and then come up with questions or comments. If you have a conversation with that employee, hold a follow-up conversation a week or so later. If your employee is an extrovert and needs to talk through what you're saying, be prepared to devote the time.

Q. Should I always give feedback in private?

A. That depends on whether the feedback is positive or negative. If an employee exhibits problem behavior in front of other people, the situation can be tricky. If you reprimand him, you'll embarrass the employee and everyone around him.

But if you ignore the situation, you'll send an equally problematic message. If your employee acts out in a retail setting, for example, onlookers will interpret this to mean that your business doesn't care about customer service. This may seem like a small matter, but unhappy customers are more likely to speak out about a company than happy ones are. And the more upset they are, the louder they'll be. So, the employee issue may snowball into a business and marketing issue.

The repercussions differ if you ignore the problem in front of other employees. They may think you're a weak leader or that you treat employees unfairly—allowing some to get away with inappropriate behavior but not others. This is true of less volatile behaviors, too, such as allowing employees to come to meetings late or unprepared, especially if they don't have the necessary documents for the meeting.

What is the best course of action? Quietly remove the employee from the situation, indicating that you'll speak later. Be discreet but definite, by saying something like, "Go back to the office and meet me at my desk in ten minutes." Or, if an employee arrives late at yet another meeting, say, "Bob, can you catch up with me after the meeting? I need to talk to you," and continue with the discussion. Then, meet with your employee in a private place behind closed doors. Once there, take these steps:

1. Ask the employee to describe what happened from his or her perspective and listen closely.
2. Comment on the problems with that particular behavior.
3. Ask the employee how he or she will avoid the problem in the future.
4. Ask the employee to write a plan and email it to you, if the problem is ongoing or complex.

If the course of action doesn't require a written plan, then email the employee and underscore that he or she should resist that behavior under any circumstances. And remember to save the email.

If your employee has done something positive, praise him or her in front of your entire team or, if appropriate, your customers. You want to share good news and hope that it's contagious. In fact, that's what award ceremonies and other honors are all about—celebrating an employee's success.

Q. Should I try to get feedback from my employees, or will it undermine my power?

A. According to Ellen Tunstall, you should listen to feedback from lots of people—peers, leaders, and customers. You may be surprised: the feedback could be even better or significantly different than you think. In other cases, you may be alerted to problems with your management style that you never anticipated.

On its website, Kelly Scientific Resources, a global scientific and clinical trials staffing company, advises that you "might also have to face the fact that something you do may be a source of problems." So, the website recommends that you ask employees for feedback on whether you do the following:

- Explain company goals clearly
- Give clear job assignments
- Keep employees informed
- Understand what motivates employees
- Discuss job requirements frequently
- Recognize good performance
- Know employees' career goals and offer career advice
- Know and use employees' skills
- Provide resources to do the job
- Listen to ideas
- Credit others for their usable ideas
- Delegate important work
- Consult employees in your decisions
- Go to bat for employees
- Try to resolve disagreements and grievances

If you receive outrageous or vastly unexpected comments from your employees, don't reject them immediately. Instead, mull them over. Ask yourself how they fit the greater feedback scheme. Do one person's ideas contradict what everyone else is saying? For example, do all your employees say you encourage their professional development, while one employee says you get in the way? If so, make sure you're treating your employees equally given their talents, aspirations, and experience. In other cases, the employee may be especially insightful or better positioned to make these comments. Think them through. Discuss them with colleagues. And determine how, if at all, you're going to use them. Remember: the *best* feedback comes from learning things about yourself that you didn't know.

Experts disagree about whether you should conduct feedback sessions with employees individually, in teams, or through anonymous comments. I highly recommend that the feedback be anonymous. Here's why: you're in charge. You have the power to reward or punish, to help people move their careers ahead or stay where they are. So, naturally, they will feel reluctant to speak out directly if they have a problem with some aspect of your management. Asking them to do so will only make them feel uncomfortable and will rob both of you of the opportunity to have an open and positive exchange.

Also, be aware of cultural issues that can affect your employees' openness to giving feedback. For example, in Japan, employees believe it's inappropriate to confront or even disagree with a manager and will resist doing so even in writing. In these cases, you may ask for recommendations on the nature of the work or your department's processes but not explicit feedback about you.

Q. What is the best way to provide negative feedback or give employees bad news?

A. Here are a few recommendations for giving negative feedback.

Recommendation #1. State the positive feedback first, especially when providing feedback to good and well-intended employees. You'll establish a framework for the message and help your employee relax enough to absorb the message and accept it in the productive spirit that you intend. Get right to the point immediately—don't lead in with background.

> You did exceptional work on the Chase account this year, and we all are proud of your accomplishments. However, you will not be able to work on the Simon International account. This client requires employees with a significant accounting background, and you still need more experience in this area.

Fast, Effective Writing

At times, the positive point may not be immediately obvious. For example, you may have an employee whom your superiors turned down for a promotion against your recommendations. You should discuss their decision with them in the hopes of reconsideration, but either way, you need to get clarification about their reasoning—which might help your employee get that promotion in the future. Notice the difference between the way you position this information and the response you'll get from your employee:

Do: After meeting with Joe and Laura, I learned the reasons why you didn't get the promotion and what you can do to increase your chances in the future.

Don't: I met with Joe and Laura, and they will not agree to the promotion. They did explain why, and their points, I'm sorry to say, are irrefutable. The only way you'll get promoted is if you deal with them.

Recommendation #2. Be forward-looking—especially when addressing an employee with great potential. You'll help the employee see the advantage of recognizing and changing poor behavior and help him or her see you as an ally and a leader. Focus on the future and the rewards and possibilities his or her changed behavior can bring. Obviously, be realistic and not in any way promissory. Notice the difference in these simple examples:

Do: You need to apply the processes we've adopted as a group.

Don't: You don't follow the processes we've adopted as a group.

This approach can motivate your employees to take action—especially if you accentuate the results they'll get from changing their behavior.

Do: You need to apply the processes we've adopted as a group. This will help you cut down on the number of corrections you need to make.

Don't: You don't follow the processes we've adopted as a group. So, you need to make an unacceptable number of corrections.

Here are a few more examples:

Do	Don't
You could get a bonus next year if your sales go up by 25 percent.	You cannot get a bonus because you did not reach the 25 percent mark.
If you attend all the training sessions consecutively, your skill level should improve.	Your skill level will not improve because you keep missing the training sessions.
To get more responsibility, you need to listen to your teammates' feedback, make your deadlines, and get agreements on next steps.	Because you don't work as part of the team, you don't get more responsibilities.
I can recommend you only if your customer ratings improve.	I cannot recommend you because your customer ratings aren't high enough.

Notice that you're not using promissory language. For example, you're not saying that your employee "will" get something but "should," "could," or "may" get it. You can also use lines like these:

- Will increase the likelihood . . .
- Work to your advantage . . .
- Help you to . . .
- Be useful as you attempt to . . .
- Move the process along . . .

Recommendation #3. Avoid using unnecessarily negative words, especially if you're trying to end a dispute, give an employee bad news, or discuss sensitive issues. They detract from the forward-looking, optimistic approach that can motivate and energize employees.

Do: You must respond to requests quickly—within twenty-four hours in most cases.
Don't: You do not respond to requests quickly enough.

At times, you may have news that's not necessarily bad but not exactly what your employee wanted to hear. For example, you may have a rating system where your employee achieved a rating of 4 out of 5. Your employee may have wanted a 5, but a 4 isn't bad. Be sure that you don't sabotage the value of a 4 by saying something like, "Although you did great work, we can only give you a 4."

If the work was so great, why didn't the employee get a 5? Instead, try something like this: "Because you did great work, we gave you a 4." In this case, follow up with a game plan that a good employee is sure to appreciate: "To improve on your score even more, you can . . ."

In these situations, avoid these words as well:

- In no way
- Neglected
- Neither . . . nor
- Never
- No
- Not
- Not ever
- Unfortunately

Of course, you will find exceptions to this rule. For example, use negative words when you are requiring the employee to take an action:

> Our team can send the proposal to our customer only when you correct the mistakes on page 4.
> You can begin that project only when you complete the other one.

. . . or that support your point of view:

> I have received only one section of the proposal to review. As you know, I stated in the meeting, and in the follow-up meeting afterward, that I needed to receive the entire proposal by now.

Q. Aren't there times when I should just come out and tell them that they dropped the ball?

A. Of course—especially when the negative behavior is serious. In these cases, you could say something like this:

> In exaggerating the breadth of our services, you made false promises to the client. This is illegal, unethical, and something we never do.
>
> Under no circumstances should you refer to anyone—a client, an employee, or a colleague—in those terms.

Also, use negative words when discussing breaches that had consequences for your entire team, your clients, or anyone else. For example, you could say, "Because you didn't process the form on time, our client received his check two months late." Then go on to explain why this was a serious problem. But make sure the situation you're discussing truly deserves that level of negativity—to quote the old adage, "Choose your battles carefully."

Recommendation #4. Always support your point with specific examples, including times and dates. For example, if one of your employees was late contributing content, so your team couldn't send a proposal on time, use concrete details to support your case:

> We could not progress with the proposal until we received the timetable from you. According to our plan, you should have provided this information on the 12th but waited until the 16th, although we sent you emails and voice mails several times asking for the timetable in between.

If the problem was behavioral, you can quote other people, too. This strengthens your case and transforms an opinion—or worse, a personal assault—into a true management issue. Let's say your employee happens to be loud and argumentative. You could say something like, "You need to keep the volume down in the office." Nice idea, but your employee will probably dispute the recommendation. He isn't loud—mostly everyone else in the office is louder. So, rely on support:

> Over the past two weeks, we have received three complaints from employees in the billing department down the hall that you are speaking too loudly.
> Twice now, facilitators in the conference room next door have asked you to keep your voice down, as your were distracting the participants.

This approach leads to the next item on our list.

Recommendation #5. Refer to outside sources that dictate your feedback—formal agreements, contracts, and project plans. This reinforces the validity of your point and makes your recommendations indisputable. You are not simply entering an opinion but following important guidelines with organizational and possibly legal repercussions.

Recommendation #6. Be precise and accurate in all your comments. For example, you might tell an employee that he missed deadlines at least ten times. You didn't literally mean ten times—you were simply making a point. But if the employee was actually late four times, exaggerating undermines your authority and gives the employee well-founded cause to disagree.

Keep an accurate record of infractions, especially if you have an employee with consistent work problems; record the number of infractions, when they occurred, and under what circumstances. This strategy has another, hidden value: aside from providing clear evidence to support your case, it will help you and your employee analyze the problem and find ways of solving it.

For example, you might find that in *every* case of the missed deadlines, the employee had ample notice that the deliverable was due. Yet, your employee is never late under sudden deadlines and does a great job putting out fires. All the evidence indicates that the problem was related to time management: the employee put work with long lead times on the back burner and forgot about them until they were late.

Be sure you are accurate in these areas, as well:

- The degree of the behavior and how you measured it
- The amount of time or money involved
- The step or steps that were or were not taken correctly or at all
- Any notices or follow-ups that you or anyone else sent along, when you sent them, and how the employee responded
- Any witnesses of the event, when helpful

Q. What if I provide feedback several times and my employee *still* doesn't change?

A. If you have uncooperative employees, you will need to give them warnings with evidence of your previous discussions and examples of how the behavior still hasn't changed. Specifics about when you should give employees warnings, and the appropriate steps for doing so, depend on your company. You should check with your human resources department and read the next section on managing difficult employees.

Managing Difficult Employees

Managing difficult employees can be a test of will. Not only must you deal with unpleasant personalities and counterproductive behavior, but you have to be strategic about it. You may want to tell the obnoxious employee to shut up or the whiny employee to take a hike, but common sense and legal requirements dictate that you must be professional and figure out a way to protect your other employees so they can be productive.

Unfortunately, most managers have little to no training on how to deal with difficult employees. Throughout my career, I've run into brilliant professionals—academics, rocket scientists, researchers, mathematicians, senior executives, and CEOs—who have no idea what to do when really great, crucial employees continue to make really bad mistakes. Many are afraid and avoid confrontations altogether. Others acquiesce to these employees' demands. There are better ways to handle this problem.

Q. What is the best way to manage difficult employees?

A. Actually, there is no one way to manage a difficult employee; there are lots of effective approaches you can take, and you need to decide which is best depending on the employee and the behavior he or she needs to change. For example, if you have a passive-aggressive employee, you must address surreptitious behavior. If you have an angry or negative employee, you'll have to address the opposite— outbursts and ongoing criticisms that border on mutiny.

Regardless, you need to remember the following:

Their problems are *not* your responsibility—it's their job to change them.
You can't change their personalities.
You are responsible for managing their behavior, whether you welcome this responsibility or not.

Perhaps the best starting point is to be clear about the problem. Although employees can suffer from lots of behavior problems, the most typical are these:

- Passive-aggressive behavior
- Untidiness or other personal hygiene problems
- Tendency to gossip

- Lack of motivation
- Negativity

Be sure to realize the difference between an employee falling into a category and the *behavior* falling into a category. Determining that an employee *is* passive-aggressive or *is* negative, for example, can present difficulties for you as a manager. You start seeing your employee under this single veil and start expecting that behavior at every turn.

Worse, you start treating your employee differently by, for example, being prepared to dismiss your "negative" employee's comments or mistrusting your passive-aggressive employee. Besides, unless you're a psychiatrist, you shouldn't analyze your employees in the first place. If you are a psychiatrist, you shouldn't be managing them.

Determining that your employees *engage* in certain behaviors is different. You aren't condemning them to a generalization; you are identifying work patterns and managing them for a more productive workplace. And, as I mentioned, different behaviors require different approaches.

Q. How can I tell for sure whether an employee is passive-aggressive at work?

A. According to Mark P. Unterberg, MD, in an article published in *Mental Health and Productivity in the Workplace: A Handbook for Organizations and Clinicians* (Jeffrey P. Kahn and Alan M. Langlieb, John Wiley & Sons, 2003), the passive-aggressive employee exhibits at least four of the following traits:

- Passively resists fulfilling routine tasks
- Complains of being misunderstood and unappreciated by others
- Is sullen and argumentative

- Unreasonably criticizes and scorns authority
- Expresses envy and resentment toward those apparently more fortunate
- Voices exaggerated and persistent complaints of personal misfortune
- Alternates between hostile defiance and contrition

The passive-aggressive employee can sabotage your plans, undercut your authority, and alienate your employees from each other. Here's why: passive-aggressive employees feign agreement to everything you say—sometimes wholeheartedly—but they sabotage you behind your back through deliberate inaction. If you tell them to complete a project, they'll agree but leave the project unattended. If you tell them to show up on time, they'll nod consent and arrive late anyway.

In addition, passive-aggressive employees envision themselves as victims, and you, as the manager, are conveniently positioned as the *victimizer.* Remember, their perspective may have little to do with your management style or (at least originally) your views about them. Of course, later, the self-fulfilling principle may kick in: the employees become so difficult or unreliable that you do skip over them for important tasks and overlook them when it's time for promotions or other rewards. Are they *really* victims? Yes—but of themselves, mostly.

Q. How do I deal with a passive-aggressive employee?

A. Whether you hire passive-aggressive people or inherit them, here are some ideas that should help:

- Record everything as if your professional life depends on it— which it might. Do your employees have performance problems? Record these problems with care, and then outline the behavior you expect from them in the most objective terms possible.

- Carefully monitor the work relationships that exist between the passive-aggressive employee and other employees. This doesn't mean you should pander to the passive-aggressive employee, give him or her less work than the others, or do without this person's skill set on a project to avoid placing him or her on a team. But use common sense: If you have an intern or a new employee, don't have your passive-aggressive employee serve as a mentor. He or she will promise to show the new person the ropes, but it will never happen. Or worse, the passive-aggressive employee will pass on a negative attitude that could start the new employee off in exactly the wrong direction. Be careful—he or she might spin a negative web and drag down your other employees' morale even further.

- Because the passive-aggressive employee's power lies in shirking responsibility, get an agreement—in writing—on major tasks and even, when necessary, minor ones. When emailing instructions, for example, end the message with "Let me know if you have ideas or questions" or "Please confirm the steps we agreed on this afternoon." In some cases, create a written agreement that you both sign. Even better, get the employee to determine the solutions, steps, and other actions she should take—then she has no choice but to own the responsibility and, hopefully, fulfill it.

- At your quarterly and yearly reviews, discuss the employee's negative behavior—and be honest. Did he fulfill his professional obligations? If not, hold him accountable. Be aware: passive-aggressives are great at concocting problems that interfere with their progress. Make him take responsibility for his actions: have him record the problems in one column and strategies for overcoming each one in another. Getting this in writing serves as an informal agreement that he will take these steps.

- When assigning tasks, be clear about the steps involved in every one—as well as deadlines, outcomes, and signs of success or failure. If you give direction to the employee on the phone or in an impromptu conversation in the hall, follow up with an email—and request that the employee reply indicating that he or she understood. This will be critical to tracking the employee's behavior pattern and avoiding the typical passive-aggressive tactic of making himself or herself the victim of miscommunications, unclear directions, or *you*. Remember that your mission is not to shove your employee out of the way but to make him or her a viable contributor to the group. Clarity will prove critical to setting this person straight.

- Finally, make sure the passive-aggressive employee is distinctly included in your group for two reasons. First, these employees tend to position themselves as being singled out and, as we discussed, as victims. That strategy becomes harder if the passive-aggressive employee shares goals and responsibilities with others.

- Second, it's important that your other employees have perspective. They'll be inundated with the passive-aggressive's complaints and criticisms, which are typically unfounded and expressed behind your back. You'll prove that every employee, regardless of work style or attitude, is responsible for participating in the group and upholding his or her share of the work. You'll also prove that you, as a leader, will uphold *your* responsibilities and not be intimidated by the bad attitudes of your subordinates.

Q. How can I address the issue of personal hygiene problems without embarrassing the employee it concerns?

A. This question is always cropping up in one form or another, and managers just don't seem to know what to do about it. In our culture, we're trained not to comment on personal matters; in the workplace, you need to determine whether it's appropriate for you to address a personal issue in the first place.

The decisive point hinges on whether you're responding to a personal preference or a professional impediment. For example, if an employee wears clothing vastly inappropriate for the workplace, such as flip-flops or shorts, you should speak out. This person can't attend meetings dressed that way, will make a bad impression on customers, and doesn't adhere to your company's dress code. So, yes—say something. But, if you simply don't like the employee's style of dress, that's a different matter altogether.

Whether or not you should comment on an employee's body odor depends on whether the smell distracts other employees or clients or otherwise interferes with work. Say an employee has such a bad odor that his colleagues feel uncomfortable taking him to meetings or avoid going into his office. That interferes with the work flow and deserves mention.

Also ask yourself whether you would speak to all employees about this problem or are singling out this particular employee. Let's stay with smell for a moment. Say you have two employees who wear perfume. You like the smell of one—it's light and clean and you hardly notice it. The other employee lays it on heavy. Besides, it's so sweet-smelling that you feel as if you're in a candy factory, not an office setting. But you can't rightfully admonish one, or lay down a no-perfume policy of any sort, unless you admonish the other. Is the perfume hurting other employees? Does anyone have environmental allergies? Are they distracted? And, if so, is it documented? If others complain and give examples of how that personal issue interferes with their ability to work, you have a case.

Finally, determine whether you see a pattern. If your employee emanates an odor every so often, maybe he or she was just in a rush that morning and forgot to shower. But if the smell infests the employee's office and every room he or she enters day after day, that's different. If you see a pattern, you need to take action.

Q. Once I am certain that the problem really does affect our work lives, what should I do?

A. Begin by documenting evidence of the problem. Did other employees or clients bring the issue to your attention? If they emailed you, email a response and save the communication. If they spoke with you, record the date they contacted you and what they said. This will serve two purposes: provide evidence when you try to convince the employee that this problem really does affect others in the office, and protect you should the employee complain that he or she is being unfairly targeted.

Then, sit down with the employee and have a quiet discussion. This may be embarrassing for both of you—you can freely admit that you feel uncomfortable. Be sure to frame your points carefully. Start by mentioning the employee's value to the organization, and then explain that you're bringing up an issue to help the employee excel in his or her career. If you mention that other people have complained, be discreet. Respect their confidentiality: do not name names, the number of people who complained, or whether they work in your department or someone else's.

Be sure to discuss the problem as objectively as possible. Avoid comments like "You smell really bad" and opt for the more objective "I've noticed an odor that's coming from your office, and I wanted you to be aware of it." Place the issue in the broader context of the professional setting, and return to the issue later to make sure it has improved.

Also, keep perspective: you're a manager, not a personal counselor. There's no need for you to determine why the problem exists by saying, for example, "Your clothes are dirty" or "You obviously let your cat sleep on your clothes." Similarly, don't present a solution, whether recommending that the employee shower or that he or she put the cat outside for the night. Instead, give clear and objective evidence that the problem exists. Your employee will determine what to do. Finally, be discreet: your employee may have an illness or be taking medication that causes the smell.

Q. I've noticed that my employee has made rude sexual comments to a few of my female employees. Should I take action or let it go until they complain to me about the problem?

A. Take action. It's your duty. Speak to the employee privately, alert the female employees that you're taking action, and contact your HR department for additional suggestions. By the way, your female employees may protest that the behavior doesn't bother them, perhaps because they don't want to cause trouble. Regardless, let them know that you appreciate their input but that the employee is not following company policy and must comply.

Q. How do I handle office gossips?

A. According to Robin Dunbar, author of *Grooming, Gossip, and the Evolution of Language* (Harvard University Press, 1996), gossip can serve a positive purpose. "What characterizes the social life of humans is the intense interest we show in each other's doings," Dunbar says. "Language . . . allows us to exchange information about other people, so short-circuiting the laborious process of finding out how they behave."

However, although gossip can play a positive role in the workplace, it usually doesn't. Let me give you an example. One of my clients was a program director with a considerable number of contractors in her workforce. In fact, at times there were as many contractors as there were full-time employees. The organization was undergoing serious changes, and the morale of everyone was shaky at best.

The contract manager was a competent, outgoing woman but, alas, a gossip. She incessantly made personal attacks on employees, subordinates, and, most of all, the director. In some cases, she spread rumors about steps the organization was allegedly going to take and the ruin these steps would bring on all of them. In other cases, she would make subtle negative comments, such as saying that one employee thought the other dressed inappropriately. Although seemingly harmless, this kind of comment could erode the goodwill between employees and add stress to their relationship.

Worse, this manager attracted people with styles similar to her own, creating a virtual cyclone of negativity and half-truths, forcing more ill will into the pipeline than anyone, even in the best, most stable conditions, could ever handle. Had the manager used her conversational skills more productively and, some would argue, ethically, she could have made a positive difference—she could have prepared employees for changes, pointing to the best resources to go to for help; played up the director's assets and how the employee base could support her mission; and recommended ways in which employees could foster each other's efforts.

So, how do you address gossips? One way is to determine *why* they gossip in the first place. For example, many employees gossip because they're insecure professionally and personally. Gossip can give them an edge. It's important to remember, by the way, that these employees feel unappreciated in *any* environment, not just yours.

Similarly, by gossiping, employees can feel powerful. They can manipulate other people, control their futures, and gain an advantage for themselves—while their victims remain defenseless. Also, they mistakenly believe that gossip gets them friendship. Of course, some people are simply gossips. It's in their personality: they gossip, listen to gossip, and create gossip when none is around. Although you can't change the employee's personality, you can take measures to limit his or her behavior and control the damage.

Ultimately, gossips care what other people think—so, one way to stop or limit their behavior is to set a public precedent. Mention publicly that you know that a great deal of gossip and ill-formed rumors have been circulating in the office. Explain that gossip is negative and destructive and that it erodes trust, lowers morale, and can affect productivity. Also mention that if your employees need insights or have questions, they should go to their team leaders or you. This proclamation may not change the employees who gossip, but it will lessen the likelihood that other employees will listen to them.

Should rumors flare up, address them immediately. Or, even better, have a strong information loop that gets employees the right information when they need it. They'll have an easier time sorting through truth and fiction and will feel greater control over their work lives. This, in turn, will limit their reliance on gossip.

Q. Is it true that gossip is worse in all-female work environments?

A. Much has been written about the communication styles of men and women, and it's true that women do tend to gossip more often and in different, more personal ways than men. One reason is that women are taught to be amenable and pleasant, willing to look after other people's needs. So it's hard for some women to make demands, assert their views, and overtly take control. Instead, they find surreptitious ways of taking power—in this case, by talking. This leads to your strongest tool for de-powering gossips: a strong, healthy unit where employees have a sense of purpose and direction. If they have a point of view, they know the channels for expressing it. If they have questions, they know where to find answers.

Q. I'm a new manager, and I inherited an unmotivated workforce. What should I do?

A. Motivating employees is an issue for many managers, whether they inherited the workforce or not. Many forces can contribute to this problem, and likely they are forces beyond your control. You can counter these forces by shifting the tide to a more powerful and energetic direction.

Remember that the pressures and unpredictable demands of the workplace do resonate and influence your employees—how could they not?—but employees need an internal sense of purpose, a feeling of *mission*, to help invest them in their work and keep them motivated. Ironically, many tools that managers use to motivate employees can have the opposite effect—for example, incentives. There's no question that incentives can be nice: there are very few employees who would turn down a chance for extra time off, an invitation to participate in a great training program, or even something as simple as a better parking space. Still, these incentives, although helpful, usually create a blaze of motivation that quickly dies down. The employees simply become accustomed to the perks. To sustain their enthusiasm, you'd need to endlessly supply more and better incentives, and the well would surely dry up.

I'm not saying you shouldn't use incentives. Just recognize them for what they are: a great way to reward employees, a nice way to reinforce a positive and productive culture, and a great way to recognize employees for outstanding work. But they are not a solution if you want to inspire the lethargic or unmotivated employee.

Q. I find that employees settle into routines, stop paying attention to the requirements of the job, and then make ridiculous mistakes. What can I do about that?

A. Obviously it is important for employees to remain motivated throughout the duration of their projects. You can help them along in a number of ways, such as sending them to training sessions. But there's no better way to motivate employees than by giving them new job challenges. The jobs should be within the breadth of their skill set, of course, but should also provide new challenges. Some managers rotate positions, for example, so that employees with similar skills take on new aspects of the job.

Q. Are rewards programs effective?

A. Like incentives, rewards—such as new and more prestigious titles and plaques denoting a job well done—can prove valuable. And, as with incentives, the novelty can wear off pretty quickly. Besides, have you ever noticed that the unmotivated employees, the ones who most need an adrenaline rush, are usually the ones who sit in the back of the room, watching as everyone else gets the rewards?

Q. Are warnings and threats motivational?

A. What you're talking about, of course, is fear: the classic strategy for coercing good behavior. Grammar school teachers used it. Our parents used it. Even prison guards use it. But managers? Does fear really motivate, inspire, and ignite the response you want from lackluster employees? In specific situations, sure—especially if you're under an intense deadline and the dangers of poor performance are immediate, evident, and high.

In other cases, however, fear has numerous drawbacks. Like rewards and incentives, fear can have a temporary effect. That immediate jolt will wear down, and employees will become accustomed to the punishment or the fear of punishment. In the process, they'll likely begin to feel resentful, negative, and estranged, and these feelings undermine one of the strongest motivational forces of all: a sense of belonging. And their ill will may spread to other employees and demoralize the workforce, which is never a good thing.

But if you seriously want to demote an employee (or threaten to), you'd better have a pretty strong wall of protection around you, including specific records of his or her poor performance; an ample or more than ample number of warnings; and a clear outline from the get-go of your expectations of the employee and the employee's personal objectives and work plan. In other words, play it fair.

In other cases, you may need to punish employees by taking them off key projects, diminishing their role within the team, or denying their requests to attend conferences or meetings. But be careful: punishment can demoralize your employees, squelching whatever energy and enthusiasm they did have.

Q. What are the best ways to motivate my employees?

A. The best way to motivate your employees is to help them see the value of their contribution to something greater: your organization, your client, or your community. Don't make something up, and don't try to figure out what they want to hear—look at what's really there. Identify how your employees contribute or can contribute in a real and meaningful way.

You can connect each employee's duties, behaviors, and other contributions to the well-being of the group in the process. This will deepen the employee's sense of belonging and tap into the impulse most of us have to do our part for the team. Place the task in the context of other employees' duties. For example, if you say, "Compile the test results by Friday and get them to me," the employee is acting in a vacuum. But if you say, "Compile the test results by Friday so Jeb and I can develop the presentation on time," you're letting the employee see that the other employees rely on him or her.

Also, work to create the most positive and forward-looking environment possible: positive energy is contagious and has a remarkable effect in motivating even the most lethargic employee. Assign tasks in meetings when the entire team is present, and get feedback from team members about how they can support each individual effort. Follow up in subsequent meetings, making sure to acknowledge each employee's contributions to the group. And take many of the measures we've discussed so far—avoiding gossip, using positive language, and providing ongoing and realistic feedback.

In a more logistical sense, make sure your employees are clear about their goals. Review them regularly and follow up. Look at ways the employees succeeded, even when the measurements aren't immediately apparent. Should they fail, find clear and identifiable ways they can succeed. And for each of the major tasks you assign, be clear about the people and other processes they will affect.

Q. How should I approach employees who seem happy but don't seem to get much done?

A happy employee isn't necessarily a motivated one. For example, social butterflies may enjoy flitting from office to office for a chat, but are they motivated? Not necessarily—in fact, they could be depleting other employees' motivation. So, be sure to use specific and quantifiable language when assigning tasks and giving feedback. For example, your employee should complete status reports regularly and get them to you every Friday by noon. This level of specificity should keep the happy employee working, too.

Q. How do I handle an employee who is always negative, is constantly complaining, and disagrees with the other employees all the time?

A. Obviously, creating a positive environment can help, but negative employees may not lighten up no matter what. Their dark dispositions could be due to any number of factors, from feeling that their professional aspirations have been thwarted to an inability to handle pressure. Quite possibly they have a negative disposition in general, seeing every situation—from completing a project to feeding their cat—as a bother or potential disaster.

Sadly, these negative employees can be more destructive than you think—their negativity can create blocks on numerous fronts. In meetings they may focus primarily on what isn't being done instead of progress that's been made, or they might launch into the possibilities for calamities. Rather than move ahead in discussions, thinking up solutions and new ideas, negative employees set the pace back or slow down processes with a barrage of questions, skepticism, and indecision.

In the end, your other employees will be either annoyed or demoralized, and you will be, once again, fed up. Yet addressing the matter is difficult because you're not necessarily responding to a *behavior* per se but an attitude. And, as much as you'd like to, you simply can't tell employees how to think or feel.

However, you can influence in a number of ways. For example, at meetings, get your negative employees to look for solutions if they start dwelling on problems. Remind them of the value of a positive, productive approach. Perhaps invite a speaker for a brown-bag lunch or half-day seminar on how employees can resist negative messages and communicate more productively with each other.

By taking these steps, however indirect, you'll give the negative employees guidelines for change and create social pressure to make them resist griping. You'll also show your other employees how to approach negativity when they confront it.

Q. What should I do when an employee goes on a rant of complaints?

A. You'd be surprised how often this happens. Let's start with what you *don't* want to do, no matter how tempting: roll your eyes, half listen, interrupt, criticize the employee, or ignore the complaints altogether. The employee could be expressing valid opinions that others may be too polite, too political, or even too loyal to express openly. Besides, brushing off the employee will only aggravate the problem, and you may send an inadvertent message to other employees that you have a closed-door policy when it comes to opinions.

Instead, put a time limit on the conversation before it starts. That way, you won't be trapped in a lengthy discussion. If the employee has something useful to say, you can always meet again. If not, you won't be trapped. During the discussion, show the employee that you're considering his or her viewpoint. If you agree with some of the comments, let the employee know. This will validate the employee's sense of worth and help him or her become less defensive.

If you disagree with the comments, you need to say that as well. Just be clear, specific, and, above all, brief. As you go, be sure to maintain control. Ask the employees questions that lead to useful answers. For example, ask for remedies to whatever problem is irking them. If they don't have any, ask them to find solutions and email them to you in time for the next meeting.

Also, set parameters. If the employee wants your opinion about other employees, forget it. If he or she is casting blame, don't listen. If the employee continues to rattle off problems and complaints, blocking the chance for any semblance of a meaningful conversation, refuse to help until he or she can come up with solutions. You need to let your employees offer criticism, but you do not need to be a punching bag.

Q. What needs to happen if an employee gets angry in front of a customer?

A. Only one thing is worse than confronting an employee who is in the midst of an angry outburst: *not* confronting the employee at all. Help defuse the situation by playing the middle—straddling the line between two extreme ways of reacting. On the one hand, you may want to reprimand the employee for his inappropriate behavior. But that would only worsen the problem: you'd embarrass the employee and whoever happens to be in the room. You'd also further fuel the negative message about your organization that witnesses are likely getting.

But if you coddle the employee or indicate that the outburst was justified, you'd be sending an equally insulting, embarrassing message—only this time you'd be humiliating the customer. Instead, calmly send your employee somewhere else—to help another customer, to retrieve something from another area—whatever seems most natural and neutral. Then deal with the situation yourself.

Take an objective approach with the customer, who, most likely, will be pretty angry. Ask what happened. Try to sort through the emotion and the actions and get the real story, but most importantly, thank the customer and make sure she gets the service she requested and the Big Three:

An apology from you, the manager

A promise that this will not happen again

A little extra like a coupon or a pen—anything that will soothe the customer (discounts work especially well, if that's an option)

Then you need to confront your employee. But don't confront him—talk to him. Ask for his take on the matter in much the same way as you did the customer. Compare the facts from both of their stories to see if you can determine who was right and who was wrong. Regardless of what you determine, remind him calmly and objectively that you heard him arguing with the customer. At that point, lay down the law of good behavior and discuss his mistakes and alternative approaches if he's angry with a customer. If this behavior persists, you need to discuss the matter with your HR department and keep written records about the employee's behavior, including the date and time of the argument and specifics about what he said.

Q. What should I do when an employee is angry with me?

A. Your employees can get angry with you for many reasons. Maybe they're upset about an organizational change—something you could neither control nor expect. Maybe there was a misunderstanding between you, or maybe you had to break bad news about a layoff or an unpopular decision you were forced to make. As their manager, you represent the company and they will direct their concerns, anger, and satisfaction about their job at you.

You can't control each employee's emotional state, and it's not your job to do so. Instead, try to address any questions, concerns, or ideas as openly as possible. By creating an open environment, you'll give the employee an opportunity to express his or her anger openly and honestly and help it dissipate before it becomes an unsolvable issue.

This openness will help you stave off a related problem: employees acting out their emotions indirectly by complaining behind your back, sabotaging projects in passive-aggressive ways, and spreading false information. Besides, by being open, you give yourself the opportunity to pick up on problems before they start.

But, should anger arise (and it typically does), you can offset it by taking at least some of these steps:

1. Be alert. Notice intense gossip? Silences in meetings when employees should be stating their opinions? High absenteeism, sarcasm, and slower-than-usual productivity? You don't want to be paranoid, but anger could be building. Test the tension with a reality check: Is the pressure at work unusually high? Have you taken a stand on any issue recently? If so, you probably should trust your instinct and observation and address the anger.

2. Deal with it. This part is tricky because no one likes to address an angry person—especially when the anger is directed at you. But if you don't address the anger, it isn't likely to drift away; it could infect your entire employee base. Be brave and confront the problem head-on.

3. Timing is everything. If you have an agenda lined up for a staff meeting and an employee seems hostile or removed, should you clear the agenda to discuss the issue? What if several employees seem to be joining in? You need to use your judgment. The items on your agenda may be priorities you can't delay addressing, or you may not be prepared to address any flare-ups or hostility. If you don't address the problem at that moment,

schedule a follow-up meeting soon when everyone present can attend to discuss the problem.

4. Jump in, feelings first. Anger might be the most consuming emotion anyone can experience. Like love, it can block out people's ability to reason, listen, and understand, and they may say mean, irrational, and potentially damaging things in the heat of the moment. Address your employee's feelings. You may not be touchy-feely, and, in most cases, it's better that you aren't. But you can call attention to your employee's state of mind and recommend that he or she calm down before a conversation can begin. You should also give yourself a few minutes to let your own anger calm before you enter into a conversation, and you might want to come to the discussion with a list of talking points to help you remain relaxed and on-topic.

5. Stop and listen. Often, angry employees simply want to talk and be heard, and it's your job to listen. That means letting them finish their sentences without interruption. Then, once they're finished, check to make sure you got their meaning right. Repeat what they said. Ask questions for clarification. Did they pile up points? If so, take brief notes so you can refer to each point later. Feel lost along the way? If so, interrupt and make sure you're accurately following the discussion. It shows that you're listening.

6. Say what you think. Be objective and rely on specific incidents and outcomes to support your point. Try to leave your emotions at the door. Unless the employee was rude or in any way abusive, treat the complaints as a business problem that needs solving and nothing more. Discuss the complaints with a colleague or friend or think them through later, if necessary.

7. Come to an agreement. If you had a disagreement, make sure the fracture is healed by the end of the discussion. If the issue

happened in the past, figure out ways to avoid doing it again. If it's ongoing, make sure your employee is clear about what he must do to move ahead without incident. Make sure your comments are action-oriented and include definite, identifiable steps to avert the situation in the future. Have the employee agree to all the steps—out loud. And take notes. You'll need them later.

As always, follow up. Send an outline of whatever plans you made, decisions you reached, and steps your employees will take, and make sure your employees receive and understand your message. Ask them to identify any changes they'd like to make, and then place your email and their response securely in your files.

Managing Disabled Employees

At one time, companies' expectation of their employees was pretty clear: they hired young people and sent them off to jobs that would accommodate their backgrounds and gender. Women became nurses, HR associates (not vice presidents), and, of course, secretaries. Men, depending on their income bracket, race, and level of education, went on to fill desk jobs of increasingly greater size.

Many employees, far more than you'd imagine, were allowed to hover at the lowest rungs or not enter the system at all because of reasons that had nothing to do with their skill set. I remember my great-aunt telling me that many interviewers during the job hunts of her youth said they couldn't hire her because she was a Jew, and they did so with no apologies and no sense of the situation being unjust. (In spite of these barriers, she led a successful career, moving on to become an assistant dean at the Katherine Gibbs School in Boston.)

The workplace today is even more diverse than it was in my great-aunt's day. Employees now work for managers ten or twenty years younger than they are, and managers must adjust to employees who are their parents' age. English is no longer the only language in the U.S. workplace. Employees at all levels from intern to executive come from a multitude of backgrounds and possess a variety of interests. It's an amazing and wonderful trend, but, as with all trends, it will take a while for everyone to grow accustomed to it.

Before we move on, here's a thought to frame our conversation: a diverse workforce is unquestionably a better workforce. Employees from places outside your native country can provide new and illuminating insights into solving problems. Middle-aged or even senior employees can tap into the storehouse of their experience. And so-called disabled employees can bring insights based on their own reference points. Different viewpoints and skill sets make companies more innovative and dynamic.

Q. I know it's not PC to feel this way, but I'm not sure how to deal with my disabled employees. Do other managers feel this way, too? What can I do to feel more comfortable?

A. Certainly some managers share this discomfort or uncertainty toward people who appear "different." Don't feel bad about it or expect that you'll naturally know how to deal with it—our culture has not accepted the role of disabled employees as being integral to the workforce despite the many disabled people who have held high-profile positions, from President Franklin D. Roosevelt to physicist Stephen Hawking.

To feel more comfortable, you need to eradicate the false premises you've been taught either blatantly or subliminally about disabled people. The most powerful is the word—and concept of—*disability*. Remember: no word with the prefix *dis* can be altogether good. We *disempower* people, *disavow* any knowledge of them, and create *distance* between ourselves and others. So, when you think that someone is *disabled*, you might subconsciously minimize who they are and what their contributions could be.

But, as I said, you didn't create these prejudices. Even the American Disabilities Act, whose mission is to "provide a clear and comprehensible mandate for the elimination of discrimination . . ." against so-called disabled Americans, defines *disabilities* in the negative:

> The term "disability" means, with respect to an individual, a physical or mental impairment that substantially limits one or more of the major life activities of such an individual.

The words reinforce the sentiment that makes the ADA necessary in the first place.

Q. Three of my employees are deaf. How does this concept of eradicating my prejudices apply to them?

A. With deaf employees, having the wrong idea about their abilities can be compounded by certain workplace realities. You, like most people, probably make judgments about people depending on their communications style. So what becomes of the deaf employees who simply don't speak in English but use signing instead? They can become invisible, entities outside the fray of the hearing workplace world, their lack of language tantamount to a lack of self.

Or, as you may notice, many deaf people are strong writers but have distinct, distracting habits, such as leaving out prepositions, articles, and other small words or using verbs in unusual ways. One reason may be that the American Sign Language structure has an object-subject-predicate order—not the subject-predicate-object order of English—and dispenses with the small connecting words.

So, a deaf employee's writing, if he or she communicates in ASL, may read like this: "For work you are due late every morning, how improve? Ride bus? Sleep early nights?"

This may lead you to wonder if they're good thinkers, educated, and competent—you need to get perspective. Remember that a person's ability or inability to communicate doesn't indicate a whole lot about his or her intelligence. For example, read this message that a friend recently received concerning his request for compensation for a back injury:

> An Administrative Law Judge Order indicates you are eligible for additional temporary total disability benefits. Therefore, we are suspending your award because you should have been receiving temporary total disability benefits from 3/17/02 through 8/21/02. The previously paid permanent partial disability benefits are considered an overpayment. We are, however, making no request that the overpaid amount be recovered at this time. Instead we will deduct this amount from any permanent partial disability award that will be reinstated after your payments for temporary total disability payments stops.

Do you know what this letter means? My friend didn't, and his attorney is now trying to figure it out. Still, this style is typical of professional writing—it crops up in regulations and agreements everywhere from the State Department to health plan brochures. The rationale for the skewed language depends on who's writing it: attorneys and policy writers claim legal precedence; academics and industry experts cite complex content. But the point remains the same: communication problems do not necessarily reflect the communicator's intelligence.

The problem, of course, is that you allow prejudices like these to keep potentially good workers of all types from working for you.

Your organization—not just your disabled employees—suffers as a result. Make an effort to understand the characteristics of your deaf and disabled workers in order to understand and appreciate them.

Q. What should I do to help integrate my disabled employees into the workplace?

A. Numerous state, federal, and local laws exist that establish required ways for you to provide "reasonable accommodations" to get your disabled employees the support they need. These laws differ depending on your location, whether your employees are living at home or abroad, and countless other factors. Consult a lawyer and your HR department—they may already have policies in place.

Regardless, be aware that these "reasonable accommodations" are usually no greater than any other accommodations you make for other employees. For example, if you have deaf employees, you need to provide interpreters for meetings or ceremonies at work. But this is no more involved (or costly) than, say, providing your hearing employees with cell phones so they can communicate from the field. Often, it's only the perception of these reasonable accommodations that makes these changes seem difficult or demanding.

In addition, try to see the workplace from the disabled employee's perspective. For example, if you have a deaf employee, you need to make sure the company's alarm system has flashing lights as well as a siren. Some organizations have televisions running full-time either to alert employees to external events or to provide distractions in the lunchroom; make sure the television is closed-captioned so deaf employees can understand and at an audible volume for any blind employees you might have.

If your employees are in wheelchairs, be sure you don't have crowded corners or cramped hallways that might interfere with their mobility. Is your cafeteria arranged so they can comfortably join other employees at the tables? If you have a fire or other emergency, is there an emergency exit they can use in case the elevators shut down?

I believe it's also critical that you learn something about the disabled employees' universe. I'm not saying you should ask these employees personal questions; in fact, you shouldn't. If they want to tell you their stories, they will. But do enlighten yourself about the context of their lives. Try learning sign language—if not fluently, at least enough to communicate basic ideas and understand fundamentals of their language. Offer to have other employees learn some sign language, too.

However, the best way to determine what your employees need is to ask them. You must respect the professionalism and integrity of your disabled employees and resist the trappings of paternalism.

Q. What should I do if I suspect that an employee has a mental illness?

A. Generally speaking, that depends on the seriousness of the situation. If you notice that certain employees seem unduly agitated and you know that they've had mental problems in the past, ask how they're feeling or if they need anything. If they need help, they'll tell you. If not, let them be. Should the situation worsen, and you fear for their well-being or that of your other employees, contact your HR department.

Most likely, though, you won't know that your employees have mental illnesses even though at least 10 percent of the existing workforce does. According to Mary Blake, public health advisor for the Department of Health and Human Services in Washington, D.C., "Many employees are afraid to discuss the fact that they have a mental illness because of the stigma attached to it. Even by just disclosing it they will face other obstacles. For example, any time an employee has a bad day, the managers may say, 'Oops, there she goes.'" In addition, managers may be reluctant to give the employees increasing responsibilities, growth opportunities, and promotions.

If an employee tips you off that someone is mentally ill, says Blake: "Ask the employee how things are going. This can open the channels of direct communication about their illness. If not, even being able to admit they're having a hard time can be a way for them to deal with it."

Should an employee acknowledge that he or she is mentally ill, Blake says the most important thing you can do is ask if the employee needs any particular accommodations. For example, the employee may be sensitive to distractions, so he or she may need an environment with less stimulation—one that's set away from the hustle and bustle of everyday functions. Or the employee may need time off every week to see a doctor or get flextime if medications cause drowsiness at certain times of the day.

Regardless, you must *never* disclose information about the employee to anyone other than an HR representative. And even then, you must do so in utmost confidentiality, without using names.

Blake says: "Managers should also learn about mental health and recovery so they can do a better job of dealing with the stigma themselves. They should know the statistics. . . . For example, their fears about violence and mental illness don't line up with what the data say. And many more people with mental illness work than those who don't." Blake adds, "The data show that people with mental illness are generally good employees."

Finally, Blake offers this word of caution: "Managers do not need to address the whys of things but should deal with the behavior, instead."

Managing the Generation Gap
Q. I'm fifty-two years old and have a new crop of employees in their twenties whom I can't seem to keep motivated. Could I be experiencing a generation gap of some sort?

A. Yes—and the generation gap is becoming more of an issue than you might think. For example, plenty of baby boomers are finding that they must adjust to managers who are younger than their own children. Young professionals are rising in the ranks faster than ever, too, with a crop of VPs in their early thirties creating a collegial relationship with employees who once would have been their bosses. The fast-paced world of the Internet, mostly an enigma to the over-fifties crowd, has created an entirely new universe of doing business that younger employees live in comfortably. A generation *gap?* More like a generation *canyon.*

In terms of how you should address your younger employees, Ellen Tunstall, a retired executive who returned to the workforce to do part-time consulting work, cautions you not to treat younger employees as if they were your kids. "This approach doesn't work," she says. "Instead you need to talk with them and listen closely to their perceptions. Become aware of what that generation wants."

Among other things, you'll find the younger generation tends to be multitaskers—talking on the phone and perusing the web simultaneously is natural and not something that necessarily shows disrespect for one task or the other. Younger employees can also tap a bank of online resources you may know little about. By perusing the web, most twentysomethings can quickly access information, identify clients, and send marketing messages that reach thousands of people every day. For this reason, it's important to get your employees' feedback as you develop project plans: their ideas may be unique and valuable.

From a cultural standpoint, younger employees tend to expect more for themselves than you did. They want growth opportunities, training, and a healthy work-life balance. In fact, fewer new employees are workaholics than ever before. Does this affect their drive? In most cases, no. The balance helps them to focus more completely when they're at work. Even more startling, at least to older managers, is the young workforce's expectation that the work-place will be positive and even fun.

To understand what this means, think about the game rooms that evolved during the dot-com boom of the 1990s. Pool and Ping-Pong tables occupied conference rooms, and refrigerators full of free or cheap sodas, waters, and iced tea occupied every lunchroom. This sociability does not necessarily detract from your employees' productivity: in fact, a pleasant work environment can fuel it.

The time that employees spend in the office, though, may not be as disconcerting for you as the time they spend outside of it. While you and your peers may show up promptly at 7:30, younger employees may trickle in at 9:00 or later. This doesn't mean that they aren't working as much; but that much of their work time is at home and online. The best way to check is simple: ask. And be specific and clear when giving out assignments. Did they make their deadlines? Did they show up for meetings? If so, don't worry if they're not at work when you're sipping your second or third cup of coffee.

Q. I'm twenty-eight, and a guy who's about my dad's age is working for me. How should I handle him?

A. Your situation is increasingly common. In fact, the U.S. Census Bureau tells us that half the U.S. population will soon be more than fifty years old, and fewer younger workers will be available to replace them. This means more retirees are returning to work than ever before for reasons that can range from financial requirements to the desire for ongoing job fulfillment. This doesn't mean they're returning as full-time workers—many are consultants, contractors, and part-time employees—but they're there, and increasingly they're working for a twentysomething.

So what can you do? For starters, don't be in denial. They are older. They do have more experience. And they can come up with great ideas. So consult them—and value them—for their expertise and the range of knowledge they have acquired over time. Also, be aware that although employees differ, you need to expect the following:

- The traditional rewards and incentives system that's such a fundamental part of most managers' strategies won't resonate here. Many of these older employees have no interest in getting ahead in the corporation: they have little interest in promotions or taking on extra responsibilities. Instead, they tend to focus on the nature of the work. What will interest them most? What will bring them personal and professional satisfaction? Focus on these issues.
- Older employees value face time at work. They show up at 7:30 and work until 5:00. They tend to like person-to-person meetings, whether individually or with a group. Conference calls, web meetings, and other distance communications venues make them uncomfortable. As far as assignments go, they want to discuss what's ahead, while younger managers tend to shoot out quick emails. So, enlighten them with a project plan. Delineate the responsibilities for them, and let them know that everyone is working—whether visibly or not. Also, make yourself available for questions and face-to-face meetings.
- The older employees' relationship to technology will be different from yours. For many, the relationship just isn't there.

Sure, they may send emails, but they generally prefer conversations instead. And yes, they go online. But join chat rooms? Read blogs? Create blogs? Not so much. This isn't to say that the older employees aren't willing to learn these things—they are. But don't expect them to be naturals, at least at first, and always be willing to train them.

Finally, though, be aware of three distinct advantages to hiring older workers. First, they tend to be self-starters and more generally autonomous that younger workers. Of course, this works only if you step out of the way and give them room to move.

Second, older employees tend to be more loyal to their organization, where younger employees, as you probably know, can flit in and out of jobs every few years looking for the next best thing. Even better, older employees won't leave because the opportunities aren't there or the senior VP's office won't be available for them—they're likely not looking for advancement.

Third, senior managers can serve as great mentors for younger employees. They have the background and expertise without the ego attachment you might find in peer mentoring. Most likely, mentoring will not be in their job description, though, so rather than assume that they'll participate, ask.

Managing the Gender Gap
Q. More than half my workforce is composed of women, and I feel that I should give them equal rights but I'm not even sure what that means. How should I proceed?

A. Gender relations can be perplexing to even the most thoughtful manager, man or woman. And, as we've discussed, the best starting point is always to look at yourself. Everyone has prejudices, and, in spite of our best intentions, they can dictate how we expect others to perform.

Check your own impulses. Do you harbor feelings, however small, that women don't have the same competencies or potentials as men—even if you are a woman? And, if you are willing to open up to women's potentials, are you willing to accommodate their distinct requirements? For example, are you willing to find ways to foster your female employees' ambitions? Do you have social networks in place that they can relate to and female mentors and advisors who can serve as role models to younger employees? Do you listen closely to their feedback and requests?

Your answers could provide insights into why you may experience a disproportionate amount of turnover of your female employees. One reason could be the demands of your workplace. Many organizations require a fifty-five- to seventy-five-hour week, sometimes more, and often an enormous amount of travel locally, nationally, and globally. This can present hardships on women who are seeking a balanced lifestyle, especially if they have family demands.

Depending on your position, and your organization, some of the solutions may be in your control; others may require permission and planning from senior management. It's a battle well worth fighting and can help keep your female employees with your company and make them healthier and more productive.

Author Sylvia Ann Hewlett, an economist and the founding president of the Center for Work-Life Policy, recommends numerous solutions. One is a variety of flextime options. In an interview with Anne Nolan (Update Column, WFC Resources, June 2007), Hewlett says, "Accounting firm Ernst & Young estimates 82 percent of its employees use some type of flexibility. Two-thirds say they view flexibility as a reason for staying at or joining the firm. It's available to everyone, not just women or parents of young children, and the options include flextime, reduced-hour schedules, compressed workweeks, job sharing, telecommuting, and short-term seasonal arrangements. Increased retention has saved the firm at least $10 million annually."

It's important to remember that women, like men, don't leave a job for child-rearing issues alone. In fact, about half of all working women are either single or childless, but increasingly more need time off to care for an elderly parent or take care of a related family issue. To help keep female and male employees in your workforce, allow for family leave, telecommuting, or other options. You shouldn't be fearful of letting employees out of your sight; with careful project planning, you'll be able to track your employees' progress and determine whether they are staying on track.

Other problems may be less obvious but are still notable forces for your female workers. One is the style differences between men and women, which are so glaring that they made books like *Men Are from Mars, Women Are from Venus* smash hits. Essentially, woman value different aspects of the workforce than men do, such as forming strong relationships with high-quality colleagues, creating products and services they believe in, and contributing to a community.

These differences mean that you may need to reshape your concept of the workplace. For example, you may want to embed opportunities to assist in nonprofit ventures—from Head Start programs to homeless shelters—into your employees' schedule. Some workplaces even offer sabbaticals where employees, men and women, can take three to six months off and work on the social service projects of their choice. Or perhaps establish an in-house mentoring program, a Big Brothers-Big Sisters arrangement, or teaching opportunities in which your employee can leave work early to lead classes or after-school programs at a local school or community center.

Another challenge for managers is dealing with the maternity leave of high-performing employees. This issue is becoming more prevalent, as so many women now occupy professional positions in the workplace. When a woman has a child and is out for maternity leave, problems can spring up. For example, a smaller company may have trouble backfilling the work of a specialized employee, or other workers may resent doing the work of a new mom on paid leave. And many new mothers feel their loyalties are strained and constantly wonder if they're being a good mom *and* a good employee—which can distract them even when they're in the office.

The best way to manage this situation is to return to the basic values of the company. You must be assertive, positive, and clear that the company supports the letter and spirit of family leave. There should be no ambiguity. Maternity is part of life, and everyone in the company supports it. Then, you need to determine the best way to move forward.

Q. If I'm too friendly or complimentary to my female employees, I'm afraid I'll be accused of harassment—but I don't want to be totally impersonal, either. Are there any guidelines about the right way to interact?

A. To distinguish right from wrong, your basic premise, regardless of circumstance or emotion, is a simple one: separate work from pleasure, professional from social. Want to tell your female employee that she looks great? Forget it—that's a social comment, hardly appropriate. Want to ask her how her date went the previous night? Don't ask. Want to tell her she handled the Spencer account especially well? That comment is professional, so go ahead. If she was out sick, then yes, ask how she's feeling. But don't make comments about whether she looks pale or healthy or gained or lost weight while out.

How about when love or romantic interest kicks in? The answer: don't do it. Don't get involved. Don't even *think* about getting involved. And the reason? Asking her on a date may make her feel uncomfortable, if not upset, because it crosses professional boundaries. Besides, your role as manager will put her in an unfair position. If she says no, you may feel angry or hurt, which could affect your decisions about her role in the workplace. Besides, even if you really could walk away unscathed, she'd still question your objectivity as a boss. Of course, if she did agree to your overtures, the problem would inevitably deepen depending on where the relationship goes.

Keep anything romantic or personal out of your relationships with your female employees, and you shouldn't have to worry about harassment.

Cultural Diversity in the Workplace

Q. My employees come from a vast range of backgrounds. What is the best way to address some of the cultural differences at work?

A. The question of cultural diversity is more relevant today than ever before. In fact, over one-quarter of all Americans consider themselves part of a minority group—and that number is quickly rising. It's imperative that you make a case for valuing diversity in the workplace. Although this seems like a given, it's not; our culture is rife with cues that diversity is not okay and sameness is a requirement.

Like the language associated with so-called disabled people, you can pick up these subtle messages in even the most open, and supposedly unbiased, statements. For example, we say we need to tolerate people who are different from ourselves. Yet, *tolerance* is a word we generally reserve for annoyances that simply won't go away, whether a bad joke or an annoying itch—undesirable realities we simply can't escape. Or we say we must *accept* people who are different, but we also *accept* situations we don't like but can't escape, rather than *embracing* or *valuing* them.

I'm not advocating that you impose PC language on your discussion of a diverse workforce. But I *am* recommending that you recognize the prejudices you may carry within as you build one. As a litmus test, ask yourself these questions, and don't feel defensive, guilty, or uncomfortable in answering them:

- Do you feel impatient with people who don't speak particularly good English? If so, you may not be listening closely to what they say and are missing out on some of their contribution.
- Do you think people, including native-born Americans, are stupid or uneducated because they use incorrect grammar in writing or speaking? If so, you may miss the opportunity to develop the talents of really smart and willing employees because of a cultural bias.
- Do you get annoyed with employees who insist you say "happy holidays" instead of "merry Christmas" because they celebrate Ramadan or Chanukah? Do you mind adapting your schedule for employees who leave early on Fridays because they celebrate the Sabbath? If so, you may be foisting a personal preference into the workplace and alienating valued employees in the process.

Once you identify these prejudices, you'll be able to address them and become a more effective manager.

Q. How can I get my employees to deal with their feelings of prejudice?

A. Remember: there is a difference between feeling prejudices and acting on them. Your first step is to ensure that your employees—

and you, of course—act professionally and objectively regarding all employee interactions. Are some of your employees coming up for a promotion? Then make sure you judge their value on the merits of their accomplishments alone. Are your employees working as a team on a project? Make sure they interact according to their roles and areas of expertise.

Getting to the root of prejudice is harder—the internal values that express themselves in subtle but destructive ways. You can't force employees to give up their biases, and you shouldn't try. Nor should you try to convince your employees that all people are the same—we aren't. And that's precisely what makes a workplace strong: tapping into the range of contexts and experiences everyone brings. What you can do is help employees relate to one another and, in the process, appreciate the differences and the contributions they bring to their work.

In terms of the employees themselves, keep in mind that specific cultures have specific rules of behavior and you may need to actively help the employee acclimate to the workplace norms. For example, in some Asian nations, it is inappropriate for employees to complain or otherwise confront a boss. In many Latin American countries, the workplace culture tends to be warm with a great deal of socializing and hand-shaking. In North America, managers expect a degree of openness, whether in meetings or in notes dropped into a suggestion box, but have boundaries in terms of their social interactions.

Depending on the situation, you may need to spell out these standards directly. For example, you may need to tell the employees that their input is not only appropriate but also welcome. Also, consider sending your employees from non-English-speaking countries to ESL training if they have trouble speaking or writing in English. Traditional business writing classes probably won't help; they'll need a program that's targeted to their requirements.

Q. My company is international, and I frequently interact with colleagues and clients halfway around the world. Should I expect them to recognize the cultural differences between us, or should I change my work style when working with them?

A. Businesses are becoming increasingly global, with either a virtual or a physical presence in a range of countries. This tells us that addressing cultural issues is more than a good idea—it's a requirement. In many cases, it makes your workplace possible.

Martha Boudreau, an executive at Fleishman-Hillard International Communications—an international PR firm—has traveled extensively and regularly interacts with employees in offices around the world. According to Boudreau: "Managers must understand that the world does not operate on American business practices. . . . You must identify cultural differences right away. You can't let them creep up on you."

One starting point is to ask your HR or talent development staff to research cultural norms in whatever country you're entering. Boudreau says, "You should learn about business etiquette, including the customs for showing politeness and respect, and learn about the expectations of men and women—such as appropriate attire and when it's appropriate to shake hands or exchange business cards."

Mary Beauregard, an intercultural consultant, also suggests that you compare and contrast your expectations, given your background and values, with theirs. For example, most Americans expect an immediate response to their emails. Many believe they can walk into their CEO's office with a question. Americans also tend to feel pretty open about dispensing their opinions. But how many of these assumptions actually make sense in the culture you're entering?

One way of gleaning insights is to talk to someone from that country who's working in your office. Ask what surprised them most about your workplace. What rituals were most perplexing? Amazing? How is it different from the office they work in when in their native country? Also, says Beauregard, read. Read national publications like the *Economist*, explore websites and blogs, and read books. You'll pick up interesting and insightful information.

Beauregard stresses the importance of learning about their language. "It's important to understand the structure of the language, key phrases, and pronunciation. If you pronounce people's names and locations correctly, you'll get a great deal of respect."

Finally, try not to make judgments about the culture. "You don't have to adopt," says Beauregard, "but be able to adapt."

Managing Bosses

Q. I know it sounds crazy, but my boss is a bigger block to my department's progress than any of my employees are. What are some ways to manage her?

A. Most managers know they need to manage their employees; that's what the job is all about. But one seldom discussed and often overlooked aspect of a job is managing your own boss—typically, managers tolerate, accommodate, or, in some cases, just survive them. Your bosses wield enormous power that can affect everything from your employees' ability to get their job done to your ability to manage your clients' expectations. And unfortunately, bosses do not always use their powers for good.

Like managing difficult employees, managing difficult bosses requires a high-strategy–low-emotional approach. This doesn't mean swallowing your feelings, but you must get beyond them to clearly identify the results you want and how to get them. Here are some answers to the questions that might perplex you the most.

Q. My boss insists that every new assignment is top priority and assigns an excruciating deadline, so I'm constantly struggling to adjust my schedule and reassign my employees. What should I do?

A. Many managers confront this problem, especially when they're working in an organization that's undergoing massive changes. It could be that your boss is in rapid reactive mode, trying to adapt to financial shifts, management changes from the top, or an inept company head. It's also entirely possible that your boss has a bad memory and has forgotten all the requirements he piled on you only weeks, even days, before.

Regardless, you can use two approaches to make sense of this mess and actually be productive in the process. The first is to come prepared for all meetings with your boss with a flowchart of your projects, indicating who is responsible for what tasks and the outcomes that you intended. Should you need to add new projects to the list and reassign employees, validate that you will be stopping or delaying other projects in the process. Be specific—have the names, deadlines, and customer expectations right in front of you.

This will accomplish three things:

1. You'll remind the boss of the other priority projects, in case he's forgotten.
2. You'll give him responsibility for the changes, rather than having to incur them yourself. Should a mess hit the fan, you have a little room to duck down and let him face it.
3. You may convince him, in the process, that the existing projects are, in fact, more important than the new ones and to delay changes until later. This is especially helpful if your boss is someone who sees what's directly in front of him as being of utmost importance but misses just about everything else.

Once the meeting's over, send your boss an email restating your next steps. Follow up from time to time to update him on your progress, lest he forget yet again.

The second approach is to work with your employees about this matter. Having movable assignments with little finality or rewards can be demoralizing. Give them a big-picture view so they know that something new is pretty much always afoot. Then, reiterate that their contributions are helpful and that most projects, even when seriously delayed, will surface again.

Q. My boss is something of a bulldog—he has outbursts and can get really degrading. If he were an employee, I'd contact HR, keep a record of his behavior, and put him on probation. But because he's my boss, what can I do?

A. You don't have to put up with abuse from anyone—not insults, degrading comments, or put-downs in any form, whether in meetings in front of other people or privately in emails. As any employee should do, you need to protect yourself.

For starters, confront your boss and address the problem. Before the meeting, determine precisely the behavior you object to and one or two documented situations where it occurred. Be sure that you have absolute clarity about when it happened and who, if anyone, was there. And be exact about the words or behavior you want to see changed. Sometimes you can even give him alternative behaviors, telling him, for example, that you would prefer for him to discuss perceived shortcomings in the privacy of his office and not in front of your employees.

When possible, show him the repercussions of his behavior. For example, you could say, "After you complained about my team's contribution to the project, two employees asked to get reassigned."

Depending on your boss, you might want to highlight what you appreciate about him or her and then bring up the problem. This will set up a positive context and let your boss know that your attitude is professional and appropriate. So, you might say, "I really want the team to reach all its goals and deadlines but can accomplish this only if I have your support in front of employees." Then explain how that situation and the others like it undermine your leadership power.

If this fails or if you're not sure if his changed behavior will endure, document everything: every discussion and every case of bullying. As always, be specific. Write dates, situations, and exact comments. If you have an email, save it and keep it in your files— but not in your work files. Depending on the situation, your boss may be able to access them. Instead, keep this record safely stashed at home.

Also, rally as many supporters around you as you can. Go to your HR department and determine its policy on harassment and abuse. Consult with an attorney, whether through your company or privately. And discuss the situation with other managers. See if they overheard especially loud and disparaging scenes and ask if they've experienced similar situations with your boss. You don't want to discuss the situation with your employees, of course, except to say, if they ask, that you and the boss are working things out.

Q. My boss is unbelievably hands-off—she hides behind closed doors and appears only for meetings, and she's unable to give me any ideas or support (great evaluations, though). Should I just feel lucky she's not breathing down my neck?

A. Sounds like your hands-off boss isn't actually a boss at all. Is this lucky? Not really. Your boss's job is to get you and your team the resources you need. You may find ways of getting these resources without directly involving her—for example, you can recommend specific items or approvals you need and volunteer to get them yourself. All she'll need to do is support you, should anyone ask. Need extra funding for a project? Discuss the reasons why you need it, offer to change the budget proposal, and get it on her desk.

When discussing these issues with your boss, be careful when accentuating why you need whatever you're requesting. Be sure to highlight the most dire (yet likely) result if you don't get everything you need. If you need those approvals for additional funding, let your boss know the true cost in terms of client confidence, employee morale, and lost follow-up revenue. Or discuss the benefits: stay with what's most likely and obvious.

Also, remember to keep the ever-important paper trail. Should all go well, you deserve some of the credit, and if your efforts fail, you need to review the problems with her and hope for better returns the next time around.

Managing Clients

Q. My client keeps changing his mind about his project, which is costing us money and time and frustrating my employees. How should I handle this?

A. Your main goal must be to get your client to take ownership of the project at every stage. And the best way—possibly the *only* way—to achieve this result is to give the client choices. One option is the yes-or-no choice. Want to install a software system as part of your project for them? It's not just any software—it's incredible software that will save them hours of time and related dollars and will make organization a corporate snap. Show them the value first and then the expense; *then* ask if they want the software. Make them aware that they can say no and you'll find something just as good. That way, they'll feel as if they have full control.

Also try what I call the "positioned" approach, which is especially useful when the benefits may not be obvious. Let's get back to that software system we discussed a moment ago. In this case, you would recommend the system you most prefer and extol its benefits but also bring a few others to the table that are almost as good. Have your clients choose the one they like most. The comparison will underscore the advantages of your system and showcase that it is truly the best choice for them, but they will feel ownership for it as they made the final decision.

When possible, sandwich the option you most want the client to accept between two extremes. Now, let's say you're offering training. Here's how your options would look:

- **Option 1.** A short, feel-good session. The employees will enjoy it, and it will take only an hour—hardly any time. Will they learn? Well, yes, as much as anyone can learn in an hour. Of course, they will get resources and handouts they can use to continue their learning.

- **Option 2.** The two-day session where they learn, practice, learn, and practice and walk out with just enough knowledge and resources to demonstrate real change. The price is affordable, and the time employees spend away from the workforce is altogether manageable. (This is the option you're promoting—your clients should have an easier time accepting it when they contrast it with the other two.)

- **Option 3.** A (very expensive) one-week session where employees jump into the deep waters of learning and focus on nothing else. Sure, you want the client to accept this option. Sure, you want to train their employees for a full week and get them to focus on nothing else but what you have to teach them. But reasonable? Likely? Not really.

The trick to this strategy is that all the options make sense, but the one you prefer is clearly the most viable option. However, just because your clients made the choice on their own doesn't mean they'll stick to it. Your clients are likely confronting a dozen demands all at once. If they start to change their mind, remind them that this was their decision. You can do this subtly by saying something like this: "When do you want to schedule that seminar you chose?"

Q. What if I have to delay a project or charge more than I originally intended?

A. Changes, like so much in life that's undesirable, are inevitable. So, spare your clients the surprise and let them know that trouble may be brewing well in advance, as soon as you suspect it might be on the horizon. For example, you may say something like, "We may need two extra weeks to complete the analysis." As always, give the client a choice when possible. So, you might say, "To ensure that our analysis is comprehensive, we may need two additional weeks to complete it. But, I think it will be worth the extra time, don't you?" The client will be prepared and will have a better time accepting it. And then, if you don't need the extra time or money, it's a welcome surprise.

Q. What if I'm not sure exactly how much time I'll need?

A. If you're unsure how long a project might take, give the client a range, like three to six months. But make sure that the project will never, no matter what calamity confronts you, take more than your estimated range. In fact, always give yourself wiggle room—not so much wiggle room that your client will be distressed, but enough that you have time to solve any unforeseen problems and still finish on deadline. And be sure to update your clients about your progress—they may get resentful if they feel forgotten or out of the loop. And who can blame them? Even if the news is no news, remind the client that you're working hard and making progress.

Q. How should I approach a client who agrees to a project, thinks it's great, and is in a big hurry to get going—but then is never willing to actually start the work?

A. This is a real problem, and an expensive one. You can take a number of steps to protect yourself, but bear in mind that you can't change your clients and may just have to put up with their foibles. One issue to consider is cash flow. If you're planning on a certain amount of revenue from this client—don't. Instead, cut that amount to half, even less. Should the project—and subsequent payments— go according to plan, great. But don't bank on it. Similarly, when drafting your project plan for your employees, have a backup strategy. Be prepared to assign them other tasks should the timing get derailed, which it inevitably will.

You also need to confront the client and clearly state the problem and your needs. Yes, your employees will be available at the times you agreed on. However, they cannot be on call if the project gets delayed. If you're billing an hourly fee, then agree from the start that you'll have at least three days' notice if they plan to cancel. Finally, get a retainer for any items you must purchase up front, whether they are materials or subcontractors.

At some point, you will have to ask yourself whether all the stop-and-go is really worth it. That's especially true if the client doesn't return phone calls, assigns work and then changes the project description once you're ramped up and have committed resources, and (as seems to go with this type of behavior) fails to pay on time. Sometimes you need to know when to walk—be careful not to lose money in your effort to make it.

Chapter 3 | MANAGING TEAMS

Creating Vision, Mission, and Positioning Statements

- Why do I need a vision or mission statement?
- What is the difference between mission statements and vision statements?
- My company already has a vision and mission statement, but it really targets the corporate point of view and doesn't directly apply to, or motivate, my department. Should I develop my own?
- How do I craft helpful, effective mission and vision statements?
- Should I involve my employees in the process of creating a mission and vision statement?
- Are there specific style requirements for mission or vision statements?
- Will the necessary amount of detail make the statement too long?
- Do these statements have to be serious? Can I add humor, irony, or edge?
- What are some examples of effective mission and vision statements?
- What should I do with the mission and vision statements once they're crafted?
- How is a positioning statement different from a mission or vision statement?
- What is the best way to develop a positioning statement?

People and Positions

- I was just promoted to manager. How can I fit into this new role without alienating my coworkers—who are now my employees—and ruining my relationships with them?
- How can I get my employees to compete less and collaborate more?
- What happens if my employees drop the ball?
- I think I'm always clear when I assign tasks, but my employees never seem to know who should do what. What's happening here?
- How can I motivate my employees—especially when we have a difficult client or a boring project?

- How do I address personality conflicts within my team?
- It's hard to work with the union at my company, let alone like or trust them. How should I be dealing with them?
- Is bringing in interns a good idea?

Training Your Employees
- How important is training for my employees?
- Should I select the training for my employees or let them take whatever they choose?
- When should I discuss my employees' training needs with them?
- What classes do you think employees *must* take to become better performers?
- Is it possible to make learning part of my department's culture?

Managing teams can be a lot like managing people—each team has its own personality, ethics, and vision. Your responsibilities as manager to a team are similar, too. You must provide clear, written guidance, get agreement, create ownership of and engagement in major initiatives, and be prepared to address the inevitable crises when they occur.

Of course, unlike individual employees, teams are fragmented: your team members may have personality clashes, they may compete, and, most of all, they may vie for your attention. Balancing these many factors and staying sane and productive requires clear strategies, lots of practice, and strong intuition.

Creating Vision, Mission, and Positioning Statements

Q. Why do I need a vision or mission statement?

A. It's imperative that your team have a sense of purpose—to the community, the organization, the client, and each other. You need to articulate this direction clearly and consistently and reinforce it constantly, and you can use your vision and mission statements to do just that. Do most mission and vision statements work? Do they actually set your team in a common direction? You may expect me to say they do, but in reality, most fail; they lack the specificity and power to motivate and direct. You need to shape these messages carefully.

Q. What is the difference between mission statements and vision statements?

A. A vision statement should inspire; it looks at how things could be in the future from a positive, big-picture point of view. A vision statement can focus on everything from a feeling of well-being among your employees to a contribution to your community to a financial state—or all of these. It can be a few quick words or one or two paragraphs. And it can be literal or symbolic. Think of Herbert Hoover's 1928 campaign: "A chicken in every pot and a car in every garage." Did he really expect every household to have a chicken in every pot? All the time? The reality of the statement is absurd, but the symbolic value is profound.

A mission statement, meanwhile, directs the business purpose of your organization. It will include specifics like "Provide customers with online solutions for 95 percent of the company business, and the remaining 5 percent of the revenue will come from the boutique services." Or you can create a softer mission, such as "Develop the best possible footwear for employees who stand on their feet, and become the leading provider to food and retail outlets nationwide."

Q. My company already has a vision and mission statement, but it really targets the corporate point of view and doesn't directly apply to, or motivate, my department. Should I develop my own?

A. Actually, it's a good idea. You need to unite your employees around a concept and a clear and invigorating sense of direction where they feel they can personally contribute. So, yes, write mission and vision statements if the following statements apply to your department:

- Plays a support role or has a distinct mission from the rest of the company. For example, one of my clients was a large accounting firm with a strong and highly profitable business consulting practice. The consulting practice was edgier and more expensive and needed its own mission statement.
- Is geographically at a distance from headquarters. Your goals and circumstances, particularly the culture in which you operate, may be distinct enough to merit your own vision.
- Has embarked on a new initiative with far-reaching consequences. One client, a university, recently launched a training program for their internal supervisors and executives including their deans, chairs, and vice presidents. Their mission, and the vision of what the program could become, was distinctly different from that of the university, whose customers were students focused on building careers in the outside world.

No matter what, if you craft your own mission and vision statements, they should directly connect to the overall goals of your corporate office. For example, one of the university's missions was to better the surrounding community. So the management program had, as part of *its* mission, to provide the training so they could do so.

Q. How do I craft helpful, effective mission and vision statements?

A. Most mission and vision statements are general, the direction vague, and the content equally appropriate for a large manufacturing plant and a family-owned pizzeria. No question, companies spend a lot of time and money developing these supposedly stellar statements. They put them on posters around the office and email everyone a copy. The statements wind up decorating the walls and the first page of every new proposal but barely serve a real purpose.

If done right, though, these short, targeted words can be the heart-beat of the organization. For that to happen, you must take an honest look at the direction you want your department to take and where you realistically but optimistically see it in the future. This process should be conscious and thorough, where you tap into the key attributes of management, especially the importance of being flexible, intuitive, trusting, and a visionary. Give yourself some time to mull your direction over, review your objectives, and think it through. Then, follow these dos and don'ts:

Do: Use language that is as specific as possible, including numbers and places such as "the major cities in the Midwest" or "five new companies."

Do not: Use clichés, especially those that everyone else in your industry uses.

Do: Make sure you can use your statements to guide your direction.

Do not: Create goals that are purely wishful thinking, such as being the "best" at something.

Do: Remain focused in one clear direction.

Do not: Stray from your company's area of expertise or marketing mission.

Q. Should I involve my employees in the process of creating a mission and vision statement?

A. It's always helpful to get as much input as you can from employees, customers, and other stakeholders to confirm your insights, shape your direction, and provide new input. By involving your employees, in particular, you get them to *own* that direction and relish the rewards when they occur.

However, get your employees' input individually, and avoid writing the statements as a group—most likely, you'll get too bogged down in arguing details. I once worked with a group of writers on the mission statement for their union, and for hours, they argued about whether they should use *writer's, writers,* or *writers.'*

Here is a good process for writing your mission statement with your employees; for the vision statement, you can use similar steps that are focused on its goals:

Have your employees write a list of points they think should be included in the statement. Try not to confine them: let them write about anything from profits to outputs.

Have your employees read their lists aloud and write their points on a flipchart. You'll find that many of the items will overlap or be identical, so you probably won't get as many as you think. As with any brainstorming activity, don't reject or criticize any of them.

Weed through the list with your group, cutting points that are redundant, can be folded into a larger point, or the group thinks are helpful but not central to your reason for being. If you own a chain of automobile shops, you may want to include the goal of raising your sales by 25 percent. But you don't need to add that you want to become more profitable—that's obvious.

Collect the remaining points in a new list: you should have three or four items. If you have more, prioritize and cut the list down again. Turn this list into your mission statement.

Q. Are there specific style requirements for mission or vision statements?

A. There are specific requirements for these statements, and they are the same for both mission and vision. First, they should contain clear, accessible language that everyone within your department can easily understand and relate to. That means no jargon or other inhibiting language. Also, avoid clichés—they contain little substance and create an insincere undertone. Use specific and meaningful alternatives. For example, most mission statements say things like "We are committed to providing unmatched customer service." What does that mean? Or, to be more precise, who *doesn't* want to provide great customer service? Reveal *how* you intend to make that customer service great by specifically stating that you will respond to requests immediately, that you will send each customer a complimentary gift, or whatever else you plan on doing.

Q. Will the necessary amount of detail make the statement too long?

A. No—the detail should be intensely focused on the core elements of your work, not on the minutiae of day-to-day operations. For example, you wouldn't say that all employees should wear professional attire, answer the phones politely, and order new ink, paper, and other supplies as necessary. That's obvious. What you would say is something like, "All employees will accurately address customer requests within twenty-four hours."

Q. Do these statements have to be serious? Can I add humor, irony, or edge?

A. As long as your style resonates with your employees and is consistent with your organization's culture and brand, you can compose the statements any way you'd like.

Q. What are some examples of effective mission and vision statements?

A. Let's start with mission statements. Some are short and sweet—and surprisingly true. For example, the Disney mission is quite simply "to make people happy." And Wal-Mart, meanwhile, says they want "to give ordinary folk the chance to buy the same thing as rich people."

Other mission statements will be a paragraph long and may read like this:

> Our mission is to supply our clients with the highest-quality paper products from manufacturers around the world for the most reasonable price and to deliver all orders within one week of the request if not sooner.

The vision statement takes a far-reaching approach that looks years into the future. Here is an example:

> The Technology Supply Center will be the leading supplier of technology goods and services in the Washington area. Our client base will consist of Fortune 500 companies and will serve the community by being the driving force behind nonprofit enterprises.

Although you want to keep your vision and mission statements realistic, don't be afraid to dream big:

> Ford will democratize the automobile—Ford (early 1900s)
> Become the dominant player in commercial aircraft and bring the world into the jet age—Boeing (1950)

There's an old saying that if you can't see it, you can't have it. Or, as Albert Einstein once remarked, imagination can be more powerful than knowledge.

Q. What should I do with the mission and vision statements once they're crafted?

A. To make these statements effective, you must continuously use them. Many companies attempt to do this by posting their statements where employees can see them, both online and throughout the office. This can help, but it won't give your employees a clear direction or sense of purpose. Use these statements as reference points in meetings and in your annual and quarterly reviews. How do your achievements or plan correspond to your mission? How can your vision statement inform your decisions? Your employees need to consistently see the link between their jobs and these statements.

Q. How is a positioning statement different from a mission or vision statement?

A. A positioning statement is a three- or four-line blurb that outlines where the company stands from a marketing perspective—basically, it contains the main selling points of your brand. For instance, a car dealership might use a positioning statement that contains the line "We're the preeminent dealer of high-end import automobiles for the greater Somova Valley," as well as other points that differentiate this operation from the other car dealerships in the area.

The positioning statement informs your employees of what's distinctive about your approach, whether you're innovative, informed, or uniquely friendly. Interestingly, your employees may know that they're all of these things but not be aware of how important that is. The positioning statement helps clarify your unique and important skills to both your employees and potential customers.

Q. What is the best way to develop a positioning statement?

A. Developing a positioning statement follows a similar process to developing your mission and vision statements:

1. Determine the *true* value of your product or service to your client: do not concoct any value that may not exist or pretend one aspect of your service is better, or more sophisticated, than it really is. One way to gather this information is to have your employees discuss the feedback they've received from clients over the past year and determine the characteristics these comments have in common. Have them give as many anecdotes and examples as possible to both further validate your strengths and give you content for your marketing materials.

   You could also have someone interview your employees to see what *they* value most; typically, these characteristics reflect what your clients and other stakeholders value, too. My clients have asked me to conduct these interviews many times, and the results are always surprising. Employees from various disciplines and locations within the company usually finger the same one or two characteristics as the most valuable. If you decide to do this, make sure you consider the content in your mission and vision statements, as well.

2. Look at the competition. You should *not* try to imitate or in any way reflect your competitors' positioning, but you should sufficiently lay claim to whatever significant traits you have in common. Similarly, it's imperative that you identify where you and your competitors state the same thing in the same words and rework that portion of your statement. This common problem can destroy any possibility that your

message will be noteworthy or otherwise memorable to your customer.

For example, one of my clients, a digital marketing firm, positioned itself as energetic, innovative, and futuristic—and in a competitive study, we found out that just about everyone used these adjectives to describe themselves. However, unlike their young competitors, my client had been in business almost one hundred years and had branched into online marketing, leveraging more traditional venues. Equally important, my client was intensely customer-focused and could boast decades-long relationships with their clients. They wisely started billing themselves as savvy strategists rooted in the stability of a one-hundred-year-old firm.

3. Share the findings. Share them with your employees, whether you have five or fifty. Build them into your marketing materials, and make sure all your marketing efforts, from brochures to proposals, somehow reflect this positioning. If you're in training, use the positioning statement in your emails or build it into your logos.

People and Positions

Q. I was just promoted to manager. How can I fit into this new role without alienating my coworkers—who are now my employees—and ruining my relationships with them?

A. Paul Condon is a program director at the Eastern Management Development Center and a former organizational development consultant who oversees a project management program for new and up-and-coming managers. "The relationship doesn't have to change if you think of yourself as being part of a team," Condon says, adding that "it's important to avoid the 'us' and 'them' philosophy, especially with the people you are leading."

Still, you are going to start making decisions for the team without necessarily getting their input, and, even harder, you'll be in charge of disciplining and rewarding them. "Usually, the people you work with will understand this and respect the fact that your role is a little different," Condon says. Yet, because of the nature of your new responsibilities, Condon also cautions, "To maintain authority, you do need a certain amount of distance from the employees. . . . Ethically you need to step back, without sacrificing the collegial and cooperative atmosphere."

This distance may feel strange at first, but eventually you'll find a friendly and professional balance that works for everyone.

Q. How can I get my employees to compete less and collaborate more?

A. Employees scrambling for power is a common problem. One good way to foster a collaborative atmosphere is to take your department on an off-site trip. However, you don't want an off-site meeting where you sit around discussing issues; organize trips where something physical is involved—ropes courses, sailing, anything that puts your team in a setting that requires a distinctly different set of tools and dynamics than those at work. In the process, your employees will learn to rely on each other in new ways and interact differently. (Be sure to rely on experts to lead the endeavors—you don't want to strand the HR department on a white-water raft without a guide.)

Within the office, it's important that you create the most positive culture possible. Be sure to recognize your employees' contributions individually and as a team—this does not mean having a special award ceremony or dignifying specific employees. Just make sure you recognize everyone's accomplishments equally so they do not compete for accolades, and also emphasize what they're accomplishing as a group.

Q. What happens if my employees drop the ball?

A. Glossing over a problem or acting like nothing went wrong will, no doubt, ring false with your employees. If they drop the ball, it's your job to outline the problems that occurred, the reasons why, and what they can do to avoid that situation in the future.

If one employee is ultimately responsible for the problem, have him or her draft the outline and review it with you. Then, relay your findings to the group and get feedback about how they could help avoid the situation in the future. If the group is ultimately responsible—whether because of poor team dynamics, incorrect budget estimations, or unnecessary delays—outline the problems with them in a meeting. Put their insights and solutions on a flipchart—but don't name names or even positions. Instead, use *we* statements such as, "We should have notified the client immediately."

In the process, you'll foster a positive environment by addressing the problem, finding ways to prevent it, and providing your employees with an even greater sense of unity. This also ensures that there is no excuse for the problem to happen again.

Q. I think I'm always clear when I assign tasks, but my employees never seem to know who should do what. What's happening here?

A. You may do a good job of assigning tasks, but you should also be setting expectations of your employees and defining their expectations of you. Be concrete. If you expect your employees to get every deliverable in on time, discuss each specific project with them and when it's due. This basic project management strategy will help employees get more specific about their contributions and how they support each other. To ensure that everyone is clear and on board, discuss these expectations early on in the process and at the beginning of each new project. This will give you a chance to answer questions and clarify the usual miscommunications before they infect the work flow.

You also must address what your employees can expect from you. This is critical—if you can always answer questions via email and at the weekly staff meeting, and promise to provide feedback at the end of each month, send out a memo that says so. That way, you'll be able to take care of any and all problems at the designated times of your choice, and your employees will know when and how to approach you.

Be sure to write down the expectations for both you and your team. If you're discussing them in a meeting, put them on a simple chart that's accessible to everyone. Make a copy and email it to everyone on your team—perhaps even post it in your conference room or some other visible place. The operative word here is *accessible:* no fancy diagrams or outlines that your employees must go online to see, but something they can't help but see every day.

Remember: you must update the chart because eventually something, if not lots of things, will change. Employees must know about the changes immediately and what specific aspects of the changes apply to them. Be sure to put the changes on your chart in red or some other visible font or color, and email the chart to everyone involved immediately. Then review the changes at your next meeting. Be available to address any follow-up questions in between. If you're too busy, assign someone to handle the questions for you. Guesswork can cause extensive damage in the ranks, especially if confused employees are vying for high-profile responsibilities.

Q. How can I motivate my employees—especially when we have a difficult client or a boring project?

A. Think about what motivates you about a difficult or boring project. What benefit will it bring your client? How will it better your organization? Weave that value into your project plan and every discussion you have with employees about the project. Don't think there's anything especially significant? You may be negatively influencing your employees. You need to discover what benefits are there and focus on those benefits in your discussions.

In addition, add an undertone of urgency: do not panic or include threats, but let your employees know that their contribution will trigger a network of significant results. Some of this can derive from your tone of voice and choice of words. Rather than say, "We really need to get this done by March 4, okay?" try a more energetic approach: "March 4 is the deadline, so let's make it." It's your job to keep your employees motivated, no matter what the project.

Q. How do I address personality conflicts within my team?

A. How you solve disputes among your employees depends on the nature of the conflicts and why they exist. It's possible that one of your team members, while perfectly competent professionally, has some serious personality issues. The most common potentially disruptive employees are passive-aggressives, who consistently let the team down while pretending not to, and negative thinkers, who can bring everyone down. In this case, you need to monitor the team member carefully to ensure that he or she gets the job done with minimal disruption to others. If the problem seems serious, contact your human resources department.

If the conflict is over an isolated event, talk to the perpetrators in a private meeting. Remind them that the issues are not personal and that all of you are focused on completing the project in a highly professional manner. Then, remind them of their individual roles and responsibilities both on the team and on this specific project to further clarify matters.

Q. It's hard to work with the union at my company, let alone like or trust them. How should I be dealing with them?

A. It's important to remember that unions have many of the same goals as the companies their members work for. In fact, according to Nancy Mills of the AFL-CIO, "Managers can see the union as a partner . . . we're a real plus for them." According to Mills, "Unions are charged with the responsibility of securing the career of the members—their mission is keeping people employed. So, it's in their members' interest to make sure the employer is successful. One of the things the unions want to do is help organizations succeed."

It's important to know that each union is organized in its own way: they have different cultures and perspectives that have built up over the years. You'll need to learn more about the particular characteristics of your employees' union by reading the union contract, getting information from your HR department, or talking to your union representative.

However, all unions do have some commonalities. For example, says Mills, "One primary objective of most unions is to ensure that a basic fairness is in place regarding how employees are treated regarding pay, access to promotions, and access to support systems. . . . Unions want to defend their employees against arbitrary decisions."

One example Mills cites is the business world's current emphasis on mentoring employees. Managers, she says, must understand that what they do for one employee they must do for others, so everyone has an equal footing for success. This also ties in with a second goal of unions: to ensure that their people have jobs in the future.

In addition to learning more about your organization's union and its goals on behalf of the employees, Mills says that you can have a better relationship with the union if you:

- Make sure employees can offer their ideas about what will help the workplace without fear of punishment or retribution. This will help them feel protected and more willing to contribute good ideas and insights. You'll also stem the likelihood that you'll have to deal with mounting tensions that were not brought to your attention until they boiled over.
- Work with the union to find solutions to layoffs and downsizing such as arbitration, especially when employees have helped the organization reach its primary goals. Says Mills: "Many companies need fewer employees once the results are reached. So, if employees know they'll end up losing their jobs, why help? No one contributes to company success that leads to their personal failure."
- Understand that the collective bargaining that happens every few years helps employees feel as though they share in your organization's success; they realize they're part of the game. This can motivate them and create a more productive and healthy workplace.

Q. Is bringing in interns a good idea?

A. Interns are a great idea for a number of reasons. One is that interns can be amazing contributors to your organization. They're often energetic and curious and find the nuances of work, which employees may find tiring or dull, vastly interesting.

Jerry Liebes, chief learning officer at the Federal Communications Commission, says that another reason for interns is to carve out a superior workforce for the future. "You never know where talent will come from," he says. "We've taken in interns who are now high-level employees. It's important to bring in people with different skill sets and train all of them to succeed."

Liebes explains that to make the intern relationship really work for you and them, you must take time to sit down and talk to them about the organization right up front. "Explain what you do and how the intern fits in," Liebes explains. "Discuss their role and why it's important. Let them know how they can contribute and figure out expectations. Managers need to make an investment to reap an investment. This isn't rocket science, but it is something that people forget or overlook."

As you determine their responsibilities, be sure to give your interns meaningful work—more than relying on them to run to the copy machine. You can add to the level of responsibility incrementally, rewarding them with increasingly important, and integral, tasks. When possible, you can connect those tasks to their career path, although, says Liebes, that's not required. In fact, for many interns, their work with you will determine what that career path should be.

Training Your Employees
Q. How important is training for my employees?
A. Growth is a great motivator and the surest way to have a fresh and energized team of employees, and training is one of the best ways to help them grow. How you determine the best training for your employees is another matter. One way is to look at your company and events in the world around you: How is your field changing? What are some of the new requirements or demands your company will place on your employees? What training can you provide to ensure that your employees meet that demand?

You also need to provide training for employees so they can reach their personal goals and make their professional objectives a reality. Most organizations offer an in-house training curriculum, but adult education centers and local universities also have a range of offerings that your employees will appreciate. Learning new skills and applying them to a changing job is a great way to keep your employees happy and your company ahead of the curve.

Q. Should I select the training for my employees or let them take whatever they choose?

A. According to Liebes, it's critical that you get involved in your employees' training experience—but not by dictating what sessions they should, or shouldn't, take. Instead, sit down with them and discuss their needs. What sessions will address their weaknesses? Help them leverage their strengths? And get them on track for their professional goals and development?

Q. When should I discuss my employees' training needs with them?

A. An annual review is a great time to talk with your employees about training, but Liebes recommends that you also review the employees' training requirements on an ongoing basis. Have a problem employee? Did a stellar employee surprise you by botching up a project? Is your organization undergoing changes? Has an employee just completed a successful project and become well positioned to move forward professionally? Training can help in all these situations.

If you have employees who are struggling at work, sit down with them and find out why. Are their organizational skills an issue? Perhaps they aren't using your technology tools to their greatest advantage. Determine those areas that could use improvement, and be frank and without judgment in the process. Then, once you identify the need, take these steps:

1. Get agreement from the employees about what will help them progress—and make sure training really is the answer. If so, discuss the mode of training that will work best for them. For example, if you have employees who are in the midst of a project and can't leave the workplace for an extended time,

have them take online classes that enable them to complete a full course in the amount of time that works best for them.

2. Determine both of your expectations of the training. What benefits can you expect to realize? How can you recognize those benefits? For example, if your employee is attending customer service training, do you expect to find that he or she is spending less time with each customer because the problem is quickly resolved? Or will the employee be more self-reliant and need to call in a manager less often for support? If you don't set these expectations, the result will be a bored employee and a frustrated trainer.

3. Review what they've learned and set more goals. What support do they need from you? How will they continue to reinforce their learning? For example, if you send your employee to a project management course but don't let him or her be a team leader, you've just wasted your money.

4. Have other employees and members of your staff, as well as your own boss when appropriate, underscore the investment and give the newly trained employee more responsibility. This will encourage other employees to take training seriously and further inspire results.

Q. What classes do you think employees *must* take to become better performers?

A. No one class will make all your employees better at their jobs. One size doesn't fit all, and the right training depends on your employees' needs and contributions to the workplace.

Q. Is it possible to make learning part of my department's culture?

A. As a manager, you can facilitate a learning culture in a number of ways. Says Liebes: "Not everyone needs training. But managers should ensure that their employees complete at least one developmental activity a year, such as attending a conference, writing a white paper, or reading an article. . . . This will create a habit of professional learning."

Another way to create a learning culture is to lead by example. Have you attended an interesting forum or read a white paper that really opened your eyes? Lead a discussion with your employees about it, either as part of a meeting or during a brown-bag lunch. You could even become an instructor and hold classes for your employees and others in your organization on subject matter you know well and ways you can help them grow.

In the process, you can learn as much as the employees. For example, you will need to plan the class. This doesn't require days of effort, but you will need enough time to review the content and, even better, see how it applies to your work. Besides, your employees will ask you some hard-hitting questions that will force you to think, problem solve, and find answers on the spot.

You can also institute monthly brown-bag or lunch-and-learn sessions that focus on one issue. You can invite your employees to lead the group or bring in a visitor. Another great option is a reading group covering everything from business books to biographies of relevant and inspiring figures. Says Liebes: "We assign chapters to our employees and write discussion questions. Then we get together and address them. It really gets people thinking—it's very stimulating." If your group is pressed for time, read only as many chapters each week as you all feel comfortable with.

Finally, attend training. This task seems to present greater difficulty to managers than it does to their employees. They simply feel too busy. Once there, though, you'll find that the information will help you function more smoothly—but you'll also get something more. After all the time you spend doling out information, giving advice, answering questions, and so on, training is a time when you can refill the well and get someone else to contribute to your growth. The experience is refreshing and enlightening and will make you a better manager.

Chapter 4

MANAGING COMMUNICATIONS

The Five Points of Plain Language

- Why is strong writing so important?
- What is the most important aspect of business writing?
- Is there any evidence that using plain language makes a difference?
- Why don't my employees already know how to use plain language?
- Do you think I should invest in training so my employees can improve their writing?

Writing Processes

- We frequently write in teams, especially when we have proposals or other long documents to complete. Is there any way we can create these documents so they are in the same style throughout and take less time to write?
- Our team assigns each person a section to write and then sends the draft to a project manager to compile. Unfortunately, the results are less than stellar. How can we make the writing work?
- One of my biggest problems is getting information to the people who need it when they need it—I know I should be able to dash off a quick email, but I'm too busy. How can I address this problem?
- What is the best way to pass along information from the higher-ups to my employees, especially if you're perpetually rushing from meeting to meeting?

Communication Vehicles

- What is the best way to send information?
- Should I avoid pull-me communications?
- Should I lay down restrictions for the word usage in my employees' emails?
- I post announcements on my company's intranet all the time, but I'm not sure anyone's checking. What can I do to drive people to my messages?

- I spent a lot of energy contributing to my company's website. How can I get people to actually visit it?
- Do people really read blogs? Should I start writing one for our website?
- CDs are cheaper to produce than brochures, and I thought it might be a good idea to prepare CDs for the next job fair. Are they effective?
- Do my employees really read our manual and policy documents?
- How do I make sure our manual is readable and comprehendible?
- I usually have my new employees spend their first few days reading the manual and other policy pieces. Is that a good idea?
- What is the best way to manage push-me communications?
- My employees are scattered all over the place—they travel, work from home, and are out in the field. What's the best way to communicate with them?

Managing interdepartmental communication may be one of the most significant and overlooked aspects of most managers' jobs today. Strong communication needs to flow through all they do—anything less and their department functions in independent pods, barely associating with each other, let alone working as a cohesive team. And the cost, in everything from billable hours to lawsuits to turnaround time, is enormous. Everything from your emails to your meetings should provide clear, concise information to your employees.

The Five Points of Plain Language
Q. Why is strong writing so important?

A. Strong writing helps your organization in many ways. Ask yourself why employees write letters, send emails, post blogs, or create manuals in the first place; if you're like most managers and employees, your answer is probably "to communicate." This is a logical answer but an incorrect one. Newspapers and magazines publish articles to communicate. Employees write to elicit a response from the recipient.

A job announcement, for example, needs to do more than simply inform potential candidates about job openings. It must get the right people to apply and keep the wrong people from wasting your time. It must help managers and human resource specialists agree on the job requirements and help applicants send the appropriate information.

With strong writing in all areas of business, you significantly increase the likelihood that you'll get the responses you want. You'll cut down on inquiries from confused employees or customers with follow-up questions, lower the likelihood of lawsuits, and increase the chances of getting your proposals approved by the higher-ups.

Then there's the training factor. When you think of training, you probably envision a room with big windows, a flipchart, and a content-savvy instructor. But every organizational communication of any merit teaches the recipient something new. A customer service manual, for example, teaches employees about policies and processes—they, in turn, teach the customers.

There's also the issue of information accessibility. Many managers believe that if the information is stored and organized on a computer network and the employees know how to access it quickly, the problem is solved. In fact, I recently met with a vice president at one of the world's largest insurance companies. His department had purchased a multimillion-dollar information management system that promised to gather, sort, and transmit information ranging from simple instructions to complex insurance policies. But while the system handled vast quantities of data, no one bothered to check the quality of the writing that was in it.

When the company's employees started using the system, they were hit by a virtual tidal wave of duplicated text, questionable content, grammatically wayward copy, and meandering logic.

The so-called communications solutions brought on communication problems of epic proportions—all because of the weak writing. Although technology can help make information accessible, it cannot make it comprehendible.

Q. What is the most important aspect of business writing?

A. Correct grammar is undeniably a crucial aspect of business writing—without it, people mistakenly think you're unintelligent or lack credibility. But what's much harder for most people is writing in plain language and making sure your employees do too.

Plain language is an international term for writing that is clear, honest, and accessible. There's never a reason *not* to use plain language and hundreds of reasons why you should—accelerating the business cycle, enhancing relationships with your readers, and lowering costs of production, among them. To create a document written in plain language, you must ensure that the writing has these five qualities:

1. **The active voice.** Every sentence has two components: an actor and an action. With the active voice, you ensure that connection between actor and action is clear, typically by placing the actor first and the action second. So, for example, you might say, "Customer service representatives provide valuable information."

   The actor is "customer service representatives" and the action is "provide valuable information." Then, you can add an object who receives that action as appropriate: "Customer service representatives provide valuable information to all our customers."

   By using the active voice, you help the reader anticipate and understand your meaning. By using the passive voice—which destroys the active voice—you separate the actor and action, convolute the language, and add unnecessary words, as you can see here: "The data we need to set up your program will be gathered by our expert."

This is more understandable as "Our experts will gather the information we need to set up your program."

A second, even more common example is when you omit the actor altogether in sentences like this one: "New guidelines for customer service protocol have been drawn up and will be sent out next week." "Drawn up" and "sent out" are the actions, but who is the actor? The active version would read as follows: "Our department has drawn up new guidelines for customer service protocol and will send them next week."

2. **Concise word use.** Cutting unnecessary words (without eliminating information) can help your reader better understand and respond to your message. You can achieve this in a number of ways, but the crux of the matter is this: eliminate any words that weigh down your message and don't add substance.

   Look at this example: "Our programs are designed to allow your employees to do business with us at a time that works best for them. They can contact us any hour of the day, any day of the week throughout the entire year."

   Losing words actually emphasizes the meaning: "Our programs let your employees conduct business with us twenty-four hours a day, year-round."

3. **Consistent reader focus.** Focus on the readers' concerns and requirements and position information in a way that works best for them. You can achieve this all-important aspect of communications by using the second person *you*—a possibility

for 90 percent of your documents. Although myths abound about the second person, there's really no reason *not* to use it.

Here is a directive written in third person: "To switch their health plans, employees must contact the HR department by July 31. If employees have problems making this deadline, because of vacations or other schedule issues, they should contact their manager."

The information is remote, as if it applies to someone else. Using the second person focuses the document on the person who really needs the information—you: "To switch your health plan, you must contact the HR department by July 31. If you have problems making this deadline, because of vacations or other schedule issues, contact me."

Another important way to focus a document on the reader is to position information from the reader's perspective by addressing these questions before you write:

- What matters most to the readers?
- How will they benefit or otherwise be affected by the message?
- What is the greatest concern, fear, or reservation you must address?
- What response do they want from you?
- What response do you want from them?

For example, say you're sending an email to a vendor who claims you owe them money. However, you can't pay them unless the paperwork is completed on their end. With the reader focus, you focus on what interests them (e.g., "So you can receive your payment, please send me the completed form") instead of what interests you (e.g., "Unless I receive the completed form, I cannot process your payment").

This difference can be significant for your employees: they may get a much better response when using the reader focus with customers, vendors, and each other.

4. **Professional tone.** *Tone* is the sound of your voice when you're communicating with someone, and it often acts independently of your words. In writing, you create a tone that readers hear in their inner ear through your words, the context of your message, and even the sentence length. By using the wrong tone, you will alter the meaning of your message—even though the words and content remain the same.

   One of your greatest concerns with tone is the formality of your message. Many people believe that highly formal, highly technical language sounds more convincing and professional. Actually, the opposite is true. People interpret dense language as being bureaucratic, deliberately inaccessible, and unfriendly. So, try to relax your language in whatever way is possible.

   Notice the difference:

   - **Overly formal:** Attached is the information pertaining to our funding request. As per our conversation and reviewed in my subsequent email on May 14, the funding will be allocated to our three groups for the purpose of permanent housing construction.

   - **Formal:** I am sending the information pertaining to our funding request as we discussed on the phone and through my email on May 14. We will allocate the funding to the three groups responsible for constructing permanent housing.

- **Informal:** I'm sending along the funding information we talked about in person and virtually on May 14. As I said, we will pass along the funding to the three groups involved in constructing the permanent housing.

Another aspect of tone that's critical to your and your employees' success when writing to professionals—whether inside or outside your field—is how you handle jargon and industry terminology. Most people believe that *jargon* and *industry terminology* are synonymous, when actually they're different approaches to using words. Jargon is grammatically incorrect and essentially meaningless, as well as not specific to a particular field of work. Industry terminology is grammatically correct and easily understood by anyone in that industry. Understanding the difference and learning the optimal way to manage both of them will help you and your employees communicate better.

Taking Control of Jargon and Industry Terminology

What is jargon?

- **Jargon is not specific to your industry.** Jargon can cover more than one industry and has no specific, immediately understood meaning. You won't find jargon in your average newspaper, and you don't use jargon at home. It is ineffectual in communicating a clear message.
- **Jargon is grammatically incorrect or doesn't use common grammar.** Jargon is usually loaded with hidden verbs and other grammar problems.
- **Other words can replace it.** You can replace the jargon and still have precise meaning.
- **How you manage jargon:** Don't use it.

What is industry terminology?

- Industry terminology is specific to just your industry or one or two others.
- Industry terminology is grammatically correct.
- **No other words can replace it.** Because these words consist of formal nouns, specific procedure, or words with deep legal implication, you cannot replace them.

5. **Cohesive and well-positioned structure.** You need to position information in a clear, chronological order, placing key points in the places where readers are most likely to see them. In general, put the most important information in the first line or paragraph or in the subject line, if you're sending an email. Readers generally focus the greatest attention there. Besides, the first few lines or words make a promise for the rest of the document, indicating whether it is urgent, important, or mundane.

   So, for example, if you're sending an email to a client asking for information that will help your employees move the project along, resist titling it "Data for project." Instead, put something like "Need data for results" in the subject line. Use the body of the email or letter to state your supporting points concisely. At the end, avoid summaries and conclusions (who wants to read what they already know?) and let the piece come to its natural conclusion.

Q. Is there any evidence that using plain language makes a difference?

A. There is lots of evidence supporting the use of plain language, from the United States and many other parts of the world. Let me give you a quick example. I conducted a study for the Bureau of Alcohol, Tobacco, and Firearms (ATF) when it was part of the Department of the Treasury. ATF had recently updated the regulation standards for those who advertise and label beer into plain language. The rewrite didn't alter the content in any way and had received the green light for legal accuracy from ATF's body of attorneys. What they wanted to find out through this study was whether the rewrite would increase the likelihood that they'd get their intended response from the reader.

The study tested the language on three subjects: beer industry insiders, including industry attorneys and employees; people in related areas, primarily from the spirits industry; and nonindustry participants who had no industry experience except as consumers and had never read a regulation. The result: the three groups overall had a higher level of comprehension of the plain-language version than the original.

In addition, the participants were invited to submit written comments about the samples as they saw fit. They commented thirty times on the original version: nineteen comments were negative and ranged from "difficult to understand" to "I have no idea what that said and it is unfair to make someone read it and pretend that it makes sense."

Q. Why don't my employees already know how to use plain language?

A. The requirements of language are rapidly changing; nowadays, you must provide information faster and with more energy than ever before. Most people under the age of fifty get their news from online venues rather than from the traditional hard-copy forms. The news is faster, in short paragraphs rather than long analysis, and the writing is terse and spicy. Then there are video games, blogs, and a whole litany of virtual communications forms that send content immediately. Your average web home page has an enticing image, color, or sound, and visitors to websites generally form an opinion of that site in one-fiftieth of a second—less time than it takes to blink their eyes. They decide whether to read an email in a word or two and expect to be moved—emotionally or viscerally—within a fraction of a second.

But when you and your employees learned how to write, your teachers couldn't predict these changes to the tenets of effective writing. And, even if the changes had already set in by the time you reached high school and college, the curriculum was probably decades away from getting you the information you needed most. So, it's up to you to educate yourself, and your employees, on how to convey messages in the best way possible.

Q. Do you think I should invest in training so my employees can improve their writing?

A. Typically, managers offer their employees a smorgasbord of training options ranging from the meat-and-potatoes basic business writing to side dishes like perfect punctuation. Their intentions are great, but the results are not always effective.

One reason is that many of the trainers are businesspeople. Can they really write *well?* And, even so, do they know how to teach? Can they identify the passive voice? Tell a participant how to transform a negative message into a reader-endearing one? In many cases trainers are academics, rooted in archaic rules. Or, they're astute business writers but simply aren't ahead of the trends.

But even with the best trainer, it's unlikely that your employees' writing will improve with training alone. Sure, they return to the office with handouts, tip sheets, worksheets, and other information-packed papers, as well as lots of enthusiasm. But the enthusiasm dies within a few days, and their knowledge dies with it. According to one source, within two weeks participants lose 97 percent of the information they learn in a standard business-writing seminar.

Another problem is that employees frequently enter the seminar with zeal, anxious to rehabilitate their writing. Yet only days afterward, they realize their writing is as problematic as ever. This is because changing these habits requires time, practice, feedback, and focusing on it for weeks, even months, after the session ends. People grow disheartened, even cynical about their own abilities, and may resist any of your future attempts to provide writing help.

The low-cost, non-time-intensive solution to helping your employees produce grammatically sound, reader-friendly documents is taking an integrated approach: establish a writing center within your department or, if possible, your organization. This center can be online or an actual office and has reference and training materials as well as someone available for editing help and advice. You don't need someone full-time—just hire a contractor for a few hours a week or use a few of your employees who are willing and have the time and skills necessary. If you have a marketing or communications department, the members of this department can probably help.

Next, establish your company voice and rules of writing by developing a style guide—include real-life examples and a range of well-written templates that will help employees write faster and habituate your preferred style of writing. You can invite representatives of various areas of the company to join an editorial review board to help make decisions as needed.

Now, with supports in place, consider bringing in trainers with a clear understanding of your field, a strong background in training, and a pile of publications that proves they know their content. To ensure that the information from the sessions stick, your employees should receive one-on-one coaching sessions or editing help afterward—either with the trainer or through your writing center. These follow-up sessions should be consistent, preferably once a week, for no longer than a half hour per person so the work flow is not interrupted.

Finally, make sure that you address your employees' writing skills in your reviews. Have your employees add strong writing as part of their objectives. And make sure you know precisely how they should improve so you can realistically gauge their success.

Writing Processes

Q. We frequently write in teams, especially when we have proposals or other long documents to complete. Is there any way we can create these documents so they are in the same style throughout and take less time to write?

A. Group writing can seem like the greatest communication trap of all. On the surface, the task may seem easy enough—have a meeting and allocate pages, or assign one or two people the task of writing for the group. When the document is done, you send it to the reviewers or other people on the team for feedback. However, everyone seems to have an opinion as the writing comes in and the rewriting—and rewriting and rewriting—begins. In fact, if your boss or other department leaders are involved, the comments seem to flow from every nook and cranny of the company. The project gets delayed but isn't necessarily better.

Try taking these steps:

1. **Create a three-part plan.** Give each of your employees a specific responsibility, such as gathering information, writing the draft, or distributing it for feedback. Next, create a realistic

schedule including time for researching, writing, and rewriting the material and a list of criteria for the draft. Do you want to have specific types of support? Do you want to have a specific list of style points they need to remember? Finally, when appropriate, establish a production budget that will determine the size and style of your document. Most managers fail to apply these basic project management strategies to their written projects and wonder why the piece doesn't quite pan out.

2. **Prewrite.** This is one of the greatest time-savers of all, slashing hours or even days off cutting and pasting time. First, create a specific list of information that belongs in the document. If needed, show this list to your stakeholders or anyone else in the organization whose approval you need for the finished project, and adjust accordingly.

3. **Write and review the draft.** Once your employees have written the draft, have them send copies to other team members two or three days before the next meeting.

    This will give everyone a chance to read the material, make comments, and come prepared for a discussion. Be sure to include the list of criteria you established at the beginning of the process. This will increase the likelihood that you'll receive useful feedback.

    At the meeting, keep the discussion as brief and objective as possible by being specific.

4. **Edit.** Make concrete changes based on the group's feedback. Then, if appropriate, get a round of comments from other interested parties.

5. **Final edit and design.** Bring the final round of comments to your next meeting. Chances are, you can revise right there by tweaking a word, cutting a sentence, or adding a slice of information. Then, send your document to the graphic designer—whether someone in your committee, an in-house employee, or a contractor.

6. **Proof.** Be sure to proofread for those little punctuation problems, grammatical mishaps, and other details that undermine the professional quality of your work. Remember to proofread on the hard copy—not on the computer.

Things will also go much more smoothly if you limit the team to six or seven people. One of these people should be a professional writer, whether a company technical or marketing writer or an outside consultant. If you're lucky, that person may even write the copy. If not, she will provide helpful feedback.

Q. Our team assigns each person a section to write and then sends the draft to a project manager to compile. Unfortunately, the results are less than stellar. How can we make the writing work?

A. You can do a few things to improve the writing in this situation. First, use as many templates as possible—whether sections of documents or entire pieces. But make sure that those templates are well written, up-to-date, and in a tight, cohesive order. That means someone, whether an internal writer or a contractor, should review these pieces before they become part of your template bank.

If possible, incorporate a line or two of instruction, so your employees know exactly what information to place in each section. So, for example, in the opening section of a proposal you could write, "Write three of the benefits our company will bring the client—use bullets and start with verbs." This will help the contributor place the right information exactly where it belongs.

Then, make sure the project manager is a strong editor and can run through the copy as it comes in, standardizing the language and cutting duplicated or unnecessary points. If not, and if you don't have anyone on your staff who can do the job, send the copy to an outside proofreader. He or she can usually speed through a document quickly, sometimes needing only hours to cover ten or twenty pages, and the price is usually reasonable.

Q. One of my biggest problems is getting information to the people who need it when they need it—I know I should be able to dash off a quick email, but I'm too busy. How can I address this problem?

A. You need to establish a clear and predictable communications flow. To achieve this, you must build an internal infrastructure—even if your team consists of only five people. You can pick from numerous models, depending on your project and the nature of your team. Here are the most common among them:

- **Flat.** This is a consensus-based approach to distributing information. Typically the manager meets with employees at least once a week for a debriefing, so everyone is privy to everyone else's questions and concerns. The advantage is that employees get all the information they need on a consistent, regular basis. The downside is that employees spend valuable (and expensive) time attending meetings to get low-priority information.

- **Hierarchical.** This order is typical of most organizations where the big-picture information filters down from the top. Should employees need information, direction, or answers, they ask their supervisor or team leader. The supervisor asks the manager, who asks the VP, who asks the senior VP, and so on. Conversely, if the business is undergoing big-picture changes originating at the senior level, the senior VP tells the VP, who tells the manager, who tells the supervisor, and on down the chain of command.

The hierarchical flow, although popular, isn't always efficient. Most employees get frustrated when they don't receive immediate answers to their questions. This can be especially problematic when they're under deadline and those changes have direct effect on how they should proceed. So, they sidestep the process and consult others, from administrative assistants to executives, anyone they can find who might have an answer. In the process, your employees may step on countless toes—including yours. Or, they may consult with fellow (and equally uninformed) employees.

If you prefer the hierarchical model, here's what you must do:

- Clearly articulate the structure of the hierarchy to your team. Be clear about whom they need to contact for information. For example, if there are two management-level people, whom does the team member approach?
- Present backup plans. If the appropriate person isn't available, who's the backup person? Is there a contingency plan?
- What is the appropriate amount of time to wait before contacting the backup person?
- Determine appropriate ways of communicating. If some team members are off-site, email works well. But should team members call each other? Contact the administrative person and leave messages? What works best?

- Address which questions should be directed at higher-level personnel and how high the employee should go to get answers.

- **Point person-based.** You assign a supervisor or employee to be the point person for addressing questions and clarifying employee confusions. If you chose this model, make sure your point person isn't too swamped to handle it and can regularly respond to emails, phone calls, and knocks on the office door.

  In some cases, you must take on the role of point person, particularly if you have a small business. Or maybe you have a unique area of expertise and you're really the only resource they can trust. If so, establish times, or even rituals, for meeting with you. For example, if your door is closed, that means no one should enter no matter what. If it's halfway open, employees should listen for phone call conversations and knock. Some businesses have little cubes outside their doors: if the red side is facing out, keep out; if yellow, come in but knock first; and so on. It's worth noting that these ideas are great, but it can be a challenge to remember to use them.

  In your conversations, be sure to instruct your employees rather than merely tell them the information they need to know so that they gradually become more independent. Point them to manuals that may answer their questions. Introduce them to specialists, either online or in your office, who may be willing to discuss the issues with them. If you see the same employees asking repeat questions about a specific task, then send them to training, find a handbook, or hire someone to develop a handbook on that subject.

- **Expert-based.** With this approach, you would assign specific people as point persons for specific issues. That designation may seem obvious—the person who oversees graphic design will obviously be the one to address questions, right? But perhaps that person is unavailable. Or perhaps some of the employees are more knowledgeable than others. Be sure to document who the point person is regardless of how obvious. And make sure he or she knows to expect inquiries and has the resources necessary to address them.

Q. What is the best way to pass along information from the higher-ups to my employees, especially if I'm perpetually rushing from meeting to meeting?

A. Determine the supports that are available to you. For example, you may have an administrative person or office manager who can take notes at the meeting. Rather than send the information yourself, a near impossibility during a busy week, the support person can do it. Or maybe your organization is in flux and you need to send news flashes about the most recent updates. In this case, create an intranet page where you can post changes at your convenience. You cannot shirk this duty, but there are ways to make it easier on yourself.

Communication Vehicles
Q. What is the best way to send information?

A. Today's business world offers a plethora of options for sending and receiving information. Once upon a time we relied on letters and memos, all typed out in standard form. But now, we have phones, emails, web postings—each with its own value to the workplace and, of course, its own limitations. The option you choose depends on who will receive your document and why you are sending it.

Let's divide workplace communications into two categories—"push-me" and "pull-me." With push-me communications, you essentially push the message to the reader. Some of the push-me venues include the following:

- Meetings—virtual and face-to-face
- Training sessions
- Telephone conversations

In some ways, push-me communications are significantly easier than pull-me communications—the message will be within the recipient's reach. However, your recipient might forget the discussion or remember it differently from the way you intended. Push-me communications require follow-up to make sure the message got through and stuck.

Another hazard to the push-me style is that if you push too much at one time, calling too often or scheduling too many meetings, you'll have an avalanche effect and bury your employees or customers in too many messages. That will result in them keeping their distance, leaving emails unopened, or finding ways to avoid meetings. Minimize the number of communications, and make sure all are valuable.

Pull-me communications are even harder in terms of reaching your audience. As the name suggests, you must pull them in. Say, for example, you post your team's work schedule on the intranet. You still need to pull them into the intranet in the first place, before your message even has a chance of being effective. Your audience is present and available for discussion during a conversation; the schedule can sit on the intranet never to be read or, for that matter, thought of again.

Here are a few other pull-me venues:

- Emails
- Intranet

- Websites
- Blogs
- CDs
- Manuals

Q. Should I avoid pull-me communications?

A. Don't avoid pull-me communications—but be aware of what they require from you to be effective. The most common pull-me communication is email.

Surprisingly, emails rank as important—and difficult—messages to write, although few people recognize this. In fact, most employees don't consider emails writing at all, although they spend hours composing them every week and receive up to three hundred emails a day. As a result, the emails may be nonsensical, ineffective, or overwhelming in sheer volume alone.

Like so many things, the best way to solve the email problem is to recognize that you have one. As a manager, this means laying down policies, or at least agreements, that will help. Don't worry about being the communications police—you wouldn't let an employee speak harshly on the phone to a customer or dress inappropriately at work, and likewise, you have every right to impose email standards. Here are a few issues that you should address:

- **Who gets what.** In your communication tree, it's critical that you spell out who in your team gets what information. For example, does everyone on your team really need to know that one of the employees is leaving early on Monday to take care of her mother? Do they need to email the same information about the charity drive two, three, or even four times? It's important that you establish this information right away, or your employees could go into email overload and start ignoring messages.

- **The subject line.** Subject lines help employees determine which emails they want to read and which ones they will delete or skim quickly. They also help create a paper trail of content. Finally, subject lines inspire a particular response that can carry over into the message: an urgent-sounding subject line strikes an urgent chord in the reader; a humorous subject line brings levity and inspires a willingness to look inside but for entirely different reasons.

- **The timing.** When crises hit, people send emails. But do you know if your employees were at their desks? That they received the message? That they check their messages as regularly as they need to? So, yes, send an email if you must, but also use the more definitive push-me methods—phone calls or face-to-face meetings.

Q. Should I lay down restrictions for the word usage in my employees' emails?

A. Actually, no. You need to establish a culture of trust and respect where all your employees treat everyone in a fair, friendly, and honest way—including you. Then you'll have nothing to worry about regarding the tone of people's emails.

Q. I post announcements on my company's intranet all the time, but I'm not sure anyone's checking. What can I do to drive people to my messages?

A. My unofficial inquiry about intranets leads me to believe that employees appreciate them and actually use them. That's not to say they're looking at everything you post—or even that your employees are among the group that uses the intranet. However, you can do a number of things to pull the visitor in.

One is to ensure that every time your employees go online, they see a link to the intranet or, even better, the intranet shows up on their screen. Also, use the intranet yourself—refer to it in meetings, tell them what you've added, and, when employees ask for information you've already posted, send them there instead of explaining. This will habituate them to going online before asking you.

Finally, continuously update your portion of the intranet: that means every week, at the latest. People check websites as a way of updating themselves and expect to find new and illuminating information. After only one or two visits where they see the same old information, your visitors will stop visiting the site, no matter how hard you pull.

Q. I spent a lot of energy contributing to my company's website. How can I get people to actually visit it?

A. These wonders of the modern age are much like a house—you invite people in, and once there, they get the chance to know all about you. Most likely, your website, or your portion of the website, is primarily geared to an external visitor—which means that you have to pull, really pull, your visitors there, because you're competing with many other websites for the same visitors.

Be sure to get the necessary search words in your headers and subheads and throughout your text so that people can find your page when they're searching for products or services like yours. You may have a web maven in your company who can help. If not, hire someone. Otherwise, you risk your site, or even your portion of the site, getting lost in the web wasteland with so many other companies' sites.

Also, be sure that your site competes in terms of image use, word use, and content. These three areas really count—don't leave any of them to amateurs. You need to make sure your site is original, too. As we discussed earlier, if you're offering jobs, what makes your positions different? If you're offering a product, why should customers buy yours? Whatever the reason, make sure your website reflects how you're better and different—and be consistent in making the whole site attractive, catchy, and exciting. Remember, your visitors determine whether they like your site in one-fiftieth of a second, and you can't predict what page of it they'll land on after a Google search.

Finally—and this is the crux of the pull-me mode of communications—if you have a website, people have to know about it. Trying to find employees? Paste your website on everything you send—emails, giveaways at conferences, handouts at talks, and so on. If you're hoping to find new clients, make sure your web address is prominent on everything you send.

Q. Do people really read blogs? Should I start writing one for our website?

It's true that people read blogs and are influenced by them. They even write blogs about blogs. But the blog universe has thousands of new appearances every day—in fact, in May 2007, one search engine tracked more than 71 million of them. So, the blockbuster blogs you hear about, the ones that are shaping politics and quoted by the *New York Times*, are among the rare exceptions.

Before you start a blog, ask yourself what you hope to achieve. Is it worth the effort? How will you draw readers in? What response do you plan to get from them? If you're pretty clear that a blog will help you fulfill your mission, here's what you do.

First, keep it short. People don't have a long attention span these days—an entry of three or four paragraphs is generally plenty. Second, keep it tense. Your blog should compel the visitor to stay because it has energy, excitement, and tension. Address a relevant and pressing question from a new and stunning angle. Alert readers to issues they may not know about and should. Reveal secrets. Somehow, you must make your message compelling.

Third, figure out how you're going to let people know your blog is out there. Should you email them? Post a notice on the intranet or company home page? With all the information that comes rushing at all of us every day, you need to find compelling ways to market it.

Q. CDs are cheaper to produce than brochures, and I thought it might be a good idea to prepare CDs for the next job fair. Are they effective?

A. Plenty of managers get behind efforts to develop CDs, whether to encourage new clients to buy their service or product, show new employees the ropes, or explain processes within the workplace. Although CDs have a starlike quality about them, they require an incredible amount of pull just to get someone to take a CD from the jacket and load it into their computer. Why would people want to go to all that trouble when they can simply use Google for all the information they would ever need on a topic? Why not just ask someone for advice? You'd need a good reason to spend time and money to create a CD that, quite possibly, no one is likely to use.

Here's what you need to do if you decide to go this route: make sure your CD has something on it that the recipients really need— something that will benefit them and they can't get anywhere else. So, if you're developing a CD for a job fair, you can discuss your organization, but limit the time you do so. People aren't going to go to all the trouble of using a CD when they can get similar information on the web. Instead, you can give them a unique job search aid—perhaps interviews with employees who landed the perfect job and their (interesting) stories, or information, worksheets, or some other tool that applicants will enjoy.

Q. Do my employees really read our manual and policy documents?

A. Your organization surely has a storehouse of manuals and policy documents, maybe online, and probably in hard copy, too, but guess what—your employees rarely use them. This can create more problems than most managers think, and you should be alerted to solving them.

I learned this firsthand after conducting a study for one of my clients, a pension benefits organization that serves millions of retirees each year. Our focus was one of their core manuals. Throughout the study, we measured the participants' ability to process and act on the information, as well as their subjective views about the composition (not content) of what they read. We found that the participants were experiencing four reoccurring problems with the manual, problems that certainly affect your manuals, too.

Problem #1: New employees generally did not understand the manuals because they were too passive, too loaded with jargon and legalistic terms, and too hard to navigate. As a result, they didn't read them.

Problem #2: Employees who had been with the organization for a long time, some of them over twenty years, hadn't opened the manuals in years. They said they already knew what was in it, but in reality, the draft had gone through countless revisions. Policies change at a pretty fast clip, and employees must keep abreast of them.

Problem #3: None of the participants in the study—employees, managers, new employees, or veterans—felt they would ever use the manual for a number of reasons: they didn't want to take time to research the content; they felt the manual was too difficult to navigate; and they believed they could get more comprehensive information from other employees. As you can imagine, the employees, particularly the new ones, got their information from the employee closest to them, usually in the next cubicle. Whether these employees were up on the content, or actually understood it, was anyone's guess.

So, what does this tell you about your own manuals? Most likely, your employees aren't using them. The pull, in this case, is just too hard. But make no mistake: manuals are the single resource containing the most legally refined and accurate information on your company, and they're your shield should legal issues crop up. You need them, and you need to find a way to make them work.

Q. How do I make sure our manual is readable and comprehensible?

A. You need to check for a few issues in your manual that might interfere with your employees' ability to access this information. You should:

- Make sure the manual is well written. Odds are, it isn't. Manuals lie around like dinosaurs, some of the sections composed when people still wrote on typewriters, containing language so tired and old it could be Shakespearian English. Sadly, when employees or managers revise or update the copy, they use the same old style.
- Check the content. As you go through the existing manual, you'll probably find portions that are outdated or just plain wrong. In fact, some of the worst writing usually masks large and egregious content problems. Once you catch these problems, rewrite the text to give employees clear guidance or do it in

person or via email. You will need to get legal input for any new material.

- Make it accessible. Employees need to be able to run through the manual, easily getting the information they need. It needs to be online and must have a clear, logical order so employees know precisely where to go for the information they want. The document should be written in plain language and should be 100 percent jargon free. If you're entering words that the employees won't understand, rewrite them or define them as you go. Forget about using a glossary: it just adds an extra step, one that most readers aren't willing to take.

- Identify changes in meetings and emails. If the organization has updated or otherwise changed the manual, let your employees know. And, even though those changes will probably be housed online and be obvious to anyone who looks, pass out copies of the specific page. Then, discuss it—not for hours but for enough time that your employees or supervisors will be well acquainted with the changes, can ask questions, and will remember to apply the information to upcoming tasks.

- Use the manual on an ongoing basis. If an employee or supervisor emails or asks you a question, refer that person to the manual instead of answering the question. This will give you three benefits: (1) employees will get in the habit of using the manual instead of asking you or, worse, other employees; (2) employees will be able to remember what they've read more easily because they retain more of what they read than what they hear; and (3) you, and your other employees, will spare yourself the time and trouble involved in answering questions. Remember: you are *not* refusing to address questions about specific issues or matters not covered in the manual—just those that are.

Q. I usually have my new employees spend their first few days reading the manual and other policy pieces. Is that a good idea?

A. Actually, I recommend against it. It's unlikely that your employee will remember all—or even anything—she's read: there's simply too much information in a manual to comprehend in one reading. Besides, much of it is probably too technical, abstract, and decontextualized to matter. So, even if they could remember (which they probably couldn't) and even if they did understand the content (which is doubtful), they wouldn't have a clue how to use it.

Instead, connect your employees to a "mentor" who will walk them through the manuals and show them how to navigate the text as questions arise. The manual is meant as a problem-solving text, not as something to be read and retained.

Q. What is the best way to manage push-me communications?

A. In some ways, push-me communications are much easier than pull-me communications. The audience is present, and you can easily convey the information to them over the phone, in the conference room, or anywhere that you can read their reactions. You don't have to lure them in.

But push-me communications do have drawbacks. Let's start by discussing meetings and presentations. Employees tend to hear only one of every three words or so, and they tend to forget even more than that. It's critical that you write the major points on a flipchart or whiteboard. Also, make sure someone is on hand to take notes, whether it's an administrative support person or an employee. After the meeting, that person should email the notes to whoever should receive them.

Similarly, with one-on-one meetings, especially about a controversial or complex matter, you need to email the person afterward.

Cover all the major points or agreements that came out of the meeting. Ask that person to respond and confirm whether he or she agrees with you or wants to change something. This will protect you should related problems crop up later. If your meeting entailed decisions, email everyone who participated—not only about the outcomes but also about the steps you took to get there.

As for telephone conversations, people are spending less and less time on the phone and more and more time communicating virtually. But phone calls play a critical role in organizational communications and bring specific benefits. One of the most important advantages is the immediacy of the conversation. Remember that emails can take a long time, hours or days, to resolve the simplest issue. You know this if you've ever tried to schedule an event via email.

Phone conversations, regardless of the time frame or subject matter, give you plenty of room to explore ideas and address issues not on the agenda. In the process, you can build your professional relationships and identify common frames of reference. Regardless, you still need to follow up every call, or at least the important ones, with an email confirming all you've said.

Q. My employees are scattered all over the place—they travel, work from home, and are out in the field. What's the best way to communicate with them?

A. There's no question that virtual communications are a fact of business life, and plenty of telecommuting opportunities can prove invaluable, from conference calls to webcams. But, when you get down to it, these modes of communication are not as good as face-to-face conversations. One reason is the virtual time lapse between the time you talk and the time they respond: although only milliseconds, the delay can affect the interaction. And, at least with conference calls, you can't see each other, and important energy can become dissipated. Finally, and perhaps most importantly, a dynamic works itself into a room when people are assembled together.

So, you need to get all your employees together at least once a month in the office, where they can talk, plan, and work together. If you don't think you can afford it, you'd better save up. These reunions will make a great difference in your employees' dynamic and productivity.

- How can I estimate the amount of time each point in the project will take, particularly when so many of the stages are dependent on other tasks?
- How exact do I need to be when estimating duration times for specific tasks?
- What are some quick and easy ways to determine costs?
- We normally bill on an hourly basis, but one of our clients wants a set project fee. Unfortunately, there are too many variables for me to give a concrete number. Should I give an estimate anyway and hope they accept it?
- What role will my profit and loss statement play in these calculations?
- How important is it to factor in risk management or security issues?

Storming, Norming, Performing, and Mourning

- What is the "storming" stage of a project?
- What do I do if disaster really does hit and my employees simply aren't performing?
- How involved should I continue to be once the team starts working well together?
- Do we need to end projects in any special way?
- Most of my employees are already enmeshed in other projects when another one finally ends. How important is it that they appear for the wrap-up?
- What if the project ends on a negative note?
- Is there anything I can do to avoid projects that seem to never end?
- My team has the same project four times a month, so we just repeat the project management process to varying degrees each time. Because we're always in mid-process, we don't have any significant endings but lots of small ones. Should I still recognize them?

Whether you assign a team leader to each task, have ongoing projects, or are constantly bombarded by new ones, your primary role as a manager is to manage projects. In fact, every other aspect of your work, from managing difficult employees to communicating effectively, is ultimately all about making your projects work. You must be aware of project management strategies, be adept at identifying and using tools, and be able to plan for the stages of each project and anticipate problems.

Q. Should I be applying certain strategies as I manage the various stages of my project?

A. You're probably applying numerous strategies, to varying degrees of complexity, already—although you may not be aware that you're applying them. Regardless, it always helps to be aware of the stages involved in your project and the strategies that are available to you as you go. For example, most projects undergo five stages: forming, storming, norming, performing, and mourning.

The Crucial Forming Stage
Q. What is the forming stage?

A. The forming stage of a project takes longer and is more important than most managers think. According to Paul Condon of the project management program at the Eastern Management Development Center, and a former organizational development consultant, many managers make the mistake of *under*-planning at this critical early stage. Says Condon, "If managers plan carefully, they'll save themselves an enormous amount of trouble later."

First, though, consider whether the project is viable. You wouldn't believe how many people neglect this stage of the project and end up promising to bring impossible results, burdening their employees with unnecessary or frustrating work, and using up important resources. Before beginning a project, ask yourself these questions:

- What is the desired outcome of this project? Does it seem reasonable? Likely?

- How many resources will I need to commit to this project—in employee time and dollars?
- What are the risks involved in this project, including concrete risks like equipment and less tangible risks such as client or employee morale?
- What projects will I need to put aside to allocate appropriate resources to this one? Is this project worth the switch?

You can use a number of tools to address these questions. Some projects, particularly smaller ones, may require little to no time to determine whether they're viable, but others need more research and analysis. There are tools available that can help you outline the benefits and deficits of a project on a graph, including the "force field analysis." In this analysis, you number each attribute on a scale, usually from 1 to 5, and the final score will help you determine if the value of a project outweighs the risk involved.

The following example is from a company that is considering introducing a new product. Although this example is simple, the force field analysis is especially useful in helping you decide on highly complex projects.

Deficits	Score	Benefits	Score
Financing requires loans and tapping into line of credit	4	Sales of new product will be immediate	5
Employees will resist change	2	Existing machines can fulfill the manufacturing requirements	4
Time and expense of training employees	2	Partnership potential with local chain of stores	2
Total:	–8		+11

If you find that the negative attributes outweigh the positive ones, you have several choices. One, of course, is to meet with your boss or client and advise that they forgo the project—bring your analysis to demonstrate that the negatives are just too high. Or, you could request time to research the matter further and ensure that your predictions about the expense or the likelihood of certain risks are accurate. Or, finally, you could sit down with well-qualified employees, review the analysis, and determine alternatives that would lower your risk and increase the likelihood of rewards.

Q. At what point should I start to assemble my team?

A. Start building a team when you're sure the project is a go. You'll have numerous matters to consider at this point—be sure to add the following to your checklist:

- Is the employee currently engaged in another project? If so, how will that project be affected? Can your employee comfortably work on both?
- Do you need someone involved for the duration of the project? Perhaps you need the employee for only a brief period of time or, quite possibly, can use a contractor or support person to help instead.
- Will your employee have to travel for an extended period of time? If so, what is the availability of replacements for her other projects?
- What is your employee's level of expertise in this particular area? Is he or she skilled enough to navigate difficulties as they arise?
- Will your employee be enthusiastic about or at least welcoming of the project?
- How familiar is your employee with this client's culture and concerns?

Finally, be sure to look at the person behind the position. In other words, determine whether this person will work well with the group dynamic. Can he or she adapt to some of the demands of the project, such as travel? How well will this person interact with the client?

Q. What considerations are important for hiring contractors?

A. Contractors are becoming a staple of business life, and if you haven't already done so, you probably will need to incorporate some into one of your teams eventually. If the project is long-term, you should try to hire contractors who have longevity with the company—perhaps even those who once worked as full-time employees. If you're working on a one-time project with a unique set of requirements, look for a specialist.

Q. What is the difference between bringing in a contractor and working with a consultant?

A. A contractor picks up work that your employees are too busy to do. Often this person or organization works on long-term projects: for example, many companies contract out their HR services, sometimes having contractors fill that role for ten or even fifteen years. A consultant usually gives advice, whether on ways to fix problems with your team or maximize your success on specific tasks. Usually consultants last for the duration of the project and move on.

With anyone you bring in to help, be sure to check their references and backgrounds carefully. Don't be tempted to hire a contracting firm because of its glossy image or name brand. And hotshot consulting firms may just send you an entry-level staff person. Also, when selecting contractors, be sure to do the following:

- Interview the actual contractors who will be working on the project—not the boss or sales representative. Be as diligent as you would with a job candidate, and even review their résumés.
- Contact at least three of the firm's clients for recommendations on projects like this one. Be specific in your questions. For example, rather than ask if the contractor did a great job on the project, ask what the client's expected outcomes were and if the contractor reached them.
- Read the contract and review it with your lawyer. Make sure the language lets you slip out of the agreement as easily as you went into it.

Q. Should I outline the roles and responsibilities for my team members on each new project?

A. That depends on a number of factors. In many cases, the roles already exist—your employees are fulfilling their usual tasks on a new project. In other cases, you may need to determine roles and responsibilities particular to that project. Either way, make sure everyone on the team is aware of what they are expected to do. If you're assigning a team leader to the project, make sure he or she is intimately familiar with everyone's part on the project and is able to manage it.

Q. What should my role be on a project as a manager?

A. According to Paul Condon, "A manager or leader should do only those things that they alone can do, and delegate the rest." Some of those tasks may include the following:

- Interfacing with outside organizations
- Getting support from outsiders

- Acquiring the long-term view and vision
- Monitoring how your organization interfaces with others

You can also use a responsibility assignment matrix, or RAM. This is an easy-to-access spreadsheet of individual employees' responsibilities for specific tasks—it should indicate the level of involvement each team member has in the task and provide general information about the best contact for specific issues.

The RAM shows how each employee's role relates to the other team members' roles. Start by determining each employee's tasks, and give them a code, usually the first letter, for the sake of brevity. So, for example, you would have a project lead, or L. Many RAMS also include participant (P), accountable (A), approval required (AR), reviewer (R), and input necessary (I).

Of course, you can add any designation you like, depending on the project. So, for example, if your project involves research, you may have a lead researcher (L), a support researcher (S), a data collector (D), a copy reviewer (C), an analyst (AS), and so on.

These tasks are general—you don't want to bog down your matrix with too many assignments and the codes that go with them. Also, you need not include support staff—you may assign a fact-checker to one of your researchers, but you don't need to put that person on the chart, as the fact-checker is not a primary player.

Q. What would my RAM look like?

A. The appearance of your RAM depends on whether you design one yourself or use software that designs it for you. Here is a simple example:

Activity	Project Team Members				Others	
Phase of project	Stella Stevens	Marie Stanford	Jennifer Jones	Ken Lowe	Client's manager	Manager
Task 1	L	S				AR
Task 2			L	S	R	S
Task 3						AR
Task 4		S	L	A	R	AR
Task 5	C					AR
Task 6				A	AR	

The RAM allows you to keep track of your employees' evolving tasks throughout the project. Need to add tasks? Move people around? Record it on your RAM so everyone is aware of the change. Remember to discuss changes with either the team lead or the supervisor in charge—don't expect them to check the RAM, or any other written document, for changes.

Q. Do I need to use the RAM for every project we work on?

A. You don't need a matrix for every project, although using one can't hurt. Some of your projects will repeat for months, maybe even years, and are so familiar that you won't need to break down the tasks. For example, if you work in a manufacturing plant, your employees will probably produce the same parts over and over again throughout the years. The people might change, and the systems might operate somewhat differently, but the essentials will stay the same and so will your RAM.

Q. On the matrix, why is the manager listed as a support researcher?

A. It's important for good leaders to trust employees as well as to lead them. This gives managers an important perspective on the employees and the projects they do every day. So, whenever possible, take a backseat on the project and observe your employees and their work from that angle.

Q. Should I get the employees' agreement before assigning them to a project?

A. That depends on your circumstances. If you really need someone to get to work quickly, then just assign it. Be clear about the value of the job, the challenges that your employees will face, and the resources available to them. If you can, try to connect the position to the employees' professional objectives.

Your RAM will come in handy here. For example, you might have an employee who's an expert in a specific field, but you don't want that person to be the primary researcher on a new project in that field because he or she is already engaged in a high-level project. Instead, you can assign the primary research to a less experienced but trustworthy subordinate and make your expert a support.

Obviously, this arrangement gives less experienced employees a chance to take on new experiences and new challenges. But it also gives the senior researchers the opportunity to mentor a colleague, experience the research from a new perspective, and learn new skills.

Q. A client requested that one of my employees be on their team, but I'd already assigned that employee to an important project and couldn't pull her away. What should I do?

A. In this type of situation, give the client some options. For example, if you know when your employee will be freed up to join the team, ask the client if they want to wait. Or underscore the professional qualities of the employees on the team. Show your client the employees' résumés and invite them to meet your employees before agreeing to anything. Let the client know they always have the right of refusal: this will make them feel more in control.

Q. What are some ways I can get my client on board with our ideas for a project from the beginning and avoid confusions or disappointments later?

A. Be perfectly clear with your client about the outcome of the project and the benchmarks that indicate your progress. Be realistic. Your client may want you to make organizational changes that will save them 25 percent of their production costs in three months. Let them know if you can realistically help them cut only 20 percent of the costs and that it will take six months. Explain why, and be as factual as possible. Then, should you actually reduce costs by, say, 23 percent in five months, they'll be happy.

Q. Should I always err on the cautious side?

A. Always be cautious, but more important, be sure to manage your client's expectations. Although you don't want to sell yourself—or your outcomes—short, especially in the excitement of the early stages of the project, you don't want to set up false expectations that will only fade away later.

Q. Should I get a signed document that outlines the specific outcomes the client and I have agreed on?

A. The line between proposal and reality can shift once you get a closer look at the project. You will need to draft some sort of agreement and email it to your client, even if you discussed it in a meeting. Then get your client's approval through a return email.

At this time, you also should determine the scope of the project. Depending on the client, you may need to include various levels of detail. If you're working on a project for the federal government, for example, give *lots* of details. If you're working on an in-house job for a client who's familiar with the project, you can probably just generally describe how you'll handle it.

One of your best tools for this task is the Work Breakdown Structure (WBS), which is, essentially, a project family tree. The "parents" are your big-picture activities, and the "children" are the detailed tasks involved in accomplishing each of those activities. The structure has three levels, each increasingly more detailed. Let's say your project was to host a conference for senior-level clients from around the nation. Your WBS might look like this:

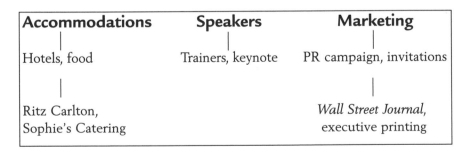

The WBS can help you for a number of reasons. According to psychologists, the human mind can comprehend no more than nine items at once. So, if you have a project with dozens of tasks, the WBS is one way to keep track. And chances are, if you're managing this project, you have lots of other projects in various stages also occupying your thoughts. Creating WBSs will help keep them all straight and let you know exactly what needs to be done.

Once you have determined the tasks, assign an employee to be responsible for them. Most likely, you already know the person who is best suited for that role—be sure to indicate it in writing, though, either on the WBS or on a separate document, to avoid confusion.

Q. How can I determine what tasks are involved in the project before it starts?

A. Base your WBS on similar projects you've worked on in the past or careful speculation—you can always go back and adapt it as things change during the project. And, most certainly, as you move forward, you or your project manager will discover new tasks and garner valuable insights that need a place on the WBS. But you must have a framework for the tasks from the beginning of the project, even if you're not 100 percent sure what they might be. A good way to approach the WBS is to start with level 1: the "parent" tasks. Next, move to level 2 and then to level 3, and don't stop until you've covered all the tasks you can think of. Be sure to double-check your estimation with your team and any other experts who can provide useful input. Your WBS is adaptable, but you shouldn't start a project without one.

Q. When do I develop a project plan, and how detailed does it need to be?

A. Actually, once you've developed your WBS, you've already started building your project plan. The plan will be as long and as complex as you need it to be. For smaller projects, you can get away with a brief plan of a few paragraphs. For larger, more complicated projects, your plan may require multiple pages. Regardless, you should include content on the following:

- Resources
- Responsibilities
- Cost
- Scope
- Time

Q. Do I need to purchase project management software? How steep is the learning curve on these types of programs?

A. Whether you need project management software is really dependent on your style, your team's experience working on projects, and the size of your organization. Smaller businesses can generally do without the sophisticated tools, whereas larger businesses usually have these systems in place, so you can just use what's already there. Whether you choose to use software or not, the most important thing to do is keep it simple. Project management has become its own industry, and simple issues or decisions that require nothing more than common sense now demand intricate technologies or complex systems.

Aside from the simplicity of the tool, you'll also need to consider the cost. You can get decent software for under $50 or sophisticated software for thousands. If you're thinking about using Gantt charts or other aids, you can download pretty good models for free online. Just google "Gantt" and click on "images." You'll be amazed at how many you can choose from.

Also, consider the complexity of your project. If you're working with partners on a large project or with employees from other departments on smaller ones, you can find online project management and collaboration tools that can help you coordinate your actions, stay abreast of your process, and indicate changes in budget, timing, or other matters. Some are free, whereas others, like Basecamphq.com, charge a small monthly fee. Or, if you need a more complex, customizable tool, check out TurboProject, Microsoft Project, and Primavera SureTrak for starters.

The simpler tools are pretty easy to use, and your learning curve should be pretty quick—usually a matter of hours. The more powerful and complicated tools are a different matter. You will need formal training either from a consultant or from an expert dedicated to project management and its tools.

Q. How can I estimate the amount of time each point in the project will take, particularly when so many of the stages are dependent on other tasks?

A. Time can be a slippery concept, and every manager knows it. With most projects, your ability to gauge time requires one part guesswork and two parts calculation—or the other way around. However, your ability to manage timing is critical to your success. To start, go back to your WBS and identify the following for every activity in your project:

- **The critical activities.** What are the tasks your employees can't perform until others are completed? For example, if you're setting up a training program, you can't develop a curriculum until you've surveyed employees and pinpointed their needs. In that case, Critical Activity #1 is taking a survey.

- **Parallel activities.** What tasks can your team do simultaneously? While you're surveying the employees, another employee could be identifying technology tools to assist in determining the right learning levels for the participants. You may also develop an adjunct time frame that factors in tasks for other projects your employees can undertake at the same time. For example, your employee may be able to draft a budget for another project while waiting for the survey results to come in.

- **The relationship between activities.** So, your team identified the sessions the employees most need to attend. Now, they need to identify the participants' level of aptitude for core subject areas. But you can't achieve that until you've identified the tool you plan to use. And you must reserve training rooms. But you can't do that until you know how many people are in each group and which rooms will accommodate that number.

- **Milestones.** How do you know you have fulfilled various stages of your project? The milestones are not the activity itself but when you complete it. For training, one milestone may be when you've finished training a level of participants. Or, it may be when those participants are able to successfully apply what they've learned based on predetermined criteria. If you're conducting research or developing a new product, you may think your milestone is when you complete a preliminary report that outlines next steps. But, actually, the *real* milestone, and the one that allows the project to move forward, will be getting approvals from the client, the senior officer, or other stake-holders. So, be clear: this will prevent you from rushing to new stages of the project too quickly.

- **Labor hours.** How many actual labor hours will you need? You may need, for example, ten hours to produce workbooks, but because copy machines work independently, you may need only a few of your employees' labor hours.

- **Duration.** How long will each activity take from inception to completion? As you mentioned earlier, you can't be exact about the duration of the task—just try to get close.

Q. How exact do I need to be when estimating duration times for specific tasks?

A. The precision of your estimates is dependent on many factors. One is whether other tasks are dependent on your completing this one. If so, you need to be exact. Another issue is the deadline. Some projects may have a floating deadline; for example, your team may need to develop a website for a client, but whether it gets up in one month or two won't make or break the site. However, if you're developing a site to generate excitement over a specific event, then exact timing will be imperative.

When determining the time frame, be sure to factor in uncertainties that may be both internally and externally generated. Internally generated problems can include employees who are out sick or crucial projects that suddenly flare up, forcing you to reassign an important employee. Or perhaps the problem lies in your estimation of steps necessary to complete a project or your employees' ability to reach certain benchmarks without external support.

Problems caused by external forces typically include budget constraints—you underestimated costs, the costs of materials went up since you initially drafted the budget, or your client estimated the wrong costs. Or your client may not have the resources or information ready as promised.

Add these and any other uncertainties you can think of into your calculation for every major task. Then, double-check your assumptions.

Will you really need a month to survey employees? Will finding trainers actually take a few weeks? Or a few months? Develop your schedule using this information. When you have a concrete, immovable deadline, you may need to strategize about ways to speed up certain stages of the process. Otherwise, err on the longer side—if you promise a result in three weeks and reach it in two, everyone's happy.

The world of project management has plenty of other ways to approach time. Some can be useful, while others are merely semantic. For example, you may give certain tasks "lag" or "lead" time where you need to wait or take preliminary steps. Here are some common ways of measuring and estimating time:

Finish to start. What tasks do you need to finish before you start new ones? If you're initiating training, you need to determine a curriculum before identifying trainers.

Start to start. Activities that start at the same time but don't end at the same time. You need to develop a web page for your training program and research and draft training materials. You'll start both projects at the same time but finish the web page first.

Finish to finish. Tasks that start at different times but must end at the same time. You may spend three months looking for trainers and three weeks developing your materials, but both must be in place before the sessions begin.

Start to finish. One task must be *finished* for another to start. You need to have trainers for the sessions to begin.

If you're using software to balance complex schedule issues, these approaches to time management will come in handy and might even be necessary for you to estimate sequences. But for smaller, less complex tasks, a straight chronology, with overlapping activities, should suffice.

Q. What are some quick and easy ways to determine costs?

A. Before estimating costs, write a list of all the resources you'll need to complete the project. Be specific and precise: if you need building tools, factor in the lumber and heavy equipment but also smaller resources such as nails. If you need to bring in outside experts, factor in related costs such as hotel fees and travel time. This point may seem logical, even obvious, but managers frequently neglect to consider those hidden costs and end up with expenses much higher than they expected.

A simple way to determine these costs is to write the obvious, typically large, resources first. This list may include any of the following:

- Labor—your employees and contractors
- Materials, including office supplies
- Warehouse or office space
- Training or related support
- Travel expenses

Now, add the less obvious or hidden resources beneath these. For example, under "training," you might write the following:

- Off-site space
- Food and snacks
- Workbooks and other support material
- Trainers

Depending on the project, you may want to break the costs down even further: the support material, for example, may include designers, production costs, and, of course, the cost of developing the content. Next, add the costs of each of these hidden expenses, and you have the total. You might end up with something like this:

- Off-site space $600
- Food and snacks ....$20 per person = $1,000
- Workbooks and other support material ..$50 per person = $2,500
- Trainers...$2,000 per day = $4,000

Be sure to give yourself a cushion, just in case. If your estimated costs tip the balance of any reasonable budget, you can strategize ways to save your company, or your client, money. For example, you may have materials from previous training that should suit your purpose just fine. Or, you may outsource the actual training to a local company and save yourself the cost of hotels and travel. Other options include training your group at the work site and sparing yourself the off-site expense, or serving sandwiches instead of a meal and spending $10 a person instead of $20.

Q. We normally bill on an hourly basis, but one of our clients wants a set project fee. Unfortunately, there are too many variables for me to give a concrete number. Should I give an estimate anyway and hope they accept it?

A. Your client probably has their own budgetary concerns, so that's generally not a good idea. You do have some options, though. For example, you can break down your expenses for the client and then build in contingency measures. Say you're in construction and are building an addition to a warehouse. You would bill a set fee for labor and material, given the parameters of the space and the type of construction. But you would also build in contingencies such as the possibility of finding rock and the cost of the material that you'd need to blast through it.

You could also provide a range. Be reasonable—say $20,000 to $25,000 and not $20,000 to $50,000. That's an unsettling discrepancy for any client. Beside the range, add a "depending" phrase, as in "Depending on the number of employees who attend the session . . ." or "Depending on the amount of rock beneath the surface . . ." That will help the client understand the discrepancy and even make choices, which will give them ownership of those choices. For example, they may decide to cap the number of employees who will attend training sessions.

Finally, you can give your client options: the more expensive options will obviously contain more services and related outcomes. Make sure you cover all your expenses for each option, adding in some wiggle room for delays or other problems.

Q. What role will my profit and loss statement play in these calculations?

A. Your past profit and loss statements (P&Ls) can actually provide you with guidelines for determining your expenses. Look for trends and hidden costs that you confronted previously, and then determine ways to avoid unpleasant surprises and cut unnecessary costs as you move forward.

If the project is large and entails complicated costs, then you should get help from a professional. Most people go to organizational strategists or project specialists, and they can certainly help, though they are pricey. You'd be amazed at how much insight your CPA or even your bookkeeper can offer, though, so consult with them, as well. Another person to consult is your banker. Bankers are experts in finance, will give you seasoned advice, and, even better, won't charge a fee. Besides, through the consultation, you'll build a relationship with your banker, which may prove helpful should you ever need a business loan.

Q. How important is it to factor in risk management or security issues?

A. It's critical that you address security issues up front. The small expense of putting in an alarm system could offset the expense of having a break-in. But you should also build a risk management plan to identify your security risks and find ways of addressing them. In fact, now is a good time to return to your force field analysis and review the risks you listed there.

Here are some of the questions you may need to address:

- What safety procedures will you adhere to? How will you monitor those procedures, and what contingency plan will you have if they fail? At what points in your project will you implement them?
- Do you plan to use contractors? If so, what process will ensure that they are not security risks—especially if you're working with highly confidential or sensitive issues? When do you plan to start investigating and hiring them?
- Do you plan to have a safety manual? What is entailed in the process of writing and dispensing it to employees?
- Will you train your employees on security procedures? What steps are involved? Who will train them? How soon into the project will that be necessary?
- Will you need to establish video surveillance? Alarm systems? Emergency telephones? At what point will you do this? How much will it cost to do so?

- Does your project require safety inspections? If so, how frequently will they occur? How will the safety inspections affect other aspects of your plan?

- Will your employees and contractors undergo drug screening tests? At what point in the project will these tests occur? Initially? As you need them?

- Will you establish an employee ID system? At what point will this occur? How will you screen employees and others working on your project?

- How about the physical location of your project? Will you have security personnel on-site? When might you need them? Will you need to restrict parking? Set up barriers of some sort?

You can also get valuable input from other companies willing to provide information that supports your interests—and theirs—for free. For example, if you're building or redesigning a facility, the utility company will flag the portions of your property that contain hidden power lines so you can stay clear and avoid power outages, fires, and worse.

Unions can advise you about ways to protect workers from fatigue or stress, which can create accidents. Citizen groups, such as citizen patrols, can help ensure your company's safety in return for a conference room where the group can meet after hours once a month. And local advocacy groups can help you identify sensitive areas of the environment that should be left undisturbed.

Finally, most insurance companies offer free help for limiting risk, including brochures, white papers, and even seminars. They cover a range of subject matter, including innovative ways to avoid break-ins, by, for example, keeping shrubs or trees around your facility trimmed or eliminating hiding places for would-be crooks. They also have plenty of information about ways to keep the workplace safe so you and your employees can avoid accidents and even fatalities at work. They also offer professional risk management services. These aren't free or cheap but could be a lot less expensive than the alternatives.

Storming, Norming, Performing, and Mourning
Q. What is the "storming" stage of a project?

A. When speaking of "storming," project management experts generally mean the relationships among your employees once the high of beginning a project has worn off and the reality of work life sinks in. If your team members have experience working on projects, they know what to expect and will take the bumps with relative calm. If not, your employees may vie for positions of influence. They may disagree about strategies. If you assign project managers, they may struggle to assert their leadership over the group. If you manage a small business or start-up, this phase can be deadly, and you may need to reassign employees or revisit your project plan.

Q. What do I do if disaster really does hit and my employees simply aren't performing?

A. According to Paul Condon, a program director at the Eastern Management Development Center, if your project plan is good and you've really looked at the many factors affecting the project, your fires should be minimal. But, should the fires flare up, Condon says that "it's important that managers develop a systemic focus: don't focus on people, but *systems*. You may think people aren't performing because they're not good people—when actually, your systems may not be supporting them."

How you address changing your systems depends on your team and your management style. You may want to debrief your project manager or key employees and then roll out the changes to your team. Or you may want to have a focus group or consensus forum where you get input on, and ownership for, the needed changes.

Regardless, Condon recommends that managers abide by the military model. He says, "The military model is to raise issues, agree with them, oppose them, and discuss them. But once you've made a decision, your team needs to get behind it . . . In the civilian world, leaders lose track of this since the issues aren't as cut-and-dry—or life-and-death. Instead, they may put on a happy face while disagreeing with it. You need to ensure you have your employees' complete commitment to the steps vital to moving ahead."

Other issues that may spring up range from employees who act out to budget overruns. We discussed these issues earlier in the book. If you find that you confront specific issues, reread the relevant sections and remember this:

- As a leader, your job is to help employees find solutions—not solve problems for them.
- Problems are a natural part of most projects. Your team needs to find productive ways of getting through them but should not feel the project is failing.
- It's important for you or your project manager to keep everyone posted about next steps or changes in the project so they can prepare for them—especially your client.
- When in mid-project, focus on moving ahead. Later, you can be introspective and figure out the lessons you have learned.

Q. How involved should I continue to be once the team starts working well together?

A. This is the famous norming and performing stage of your project, when the team gels and really starts to produce. This doesn't have to occur *after* the storming stage—and, in most cases, shouldn't. Whenever it happens, your team will eventually come together and processes will click. The manager's role is to lead employees, not to micromanage or babysit them. So, you should be able to step away and let them get their jobs done, while remaining available for updates and questions.

Q. Do we need to end projects in any special way?

A. Projects can end in two different ways. When the projects are good, the challenges intriguing, and the outcomes impressive, employees may go through a mourning period at the end. Your role, as a leader, is to help them get a sense of closure. Perhaps have a small office party or get everyone together to remind them that they did great work. You may want to sit down with key employees and give them feedback, particularly on their successes.

You also should draft documentation about the project. This will help you defend yourself should the product, service, or process you developed fail to live up to expectations, enable you to easily share information with your clients and stakeholders, and inform your employees of the strengths and weaknesses of their collective effort.

As a manager, you may not be responsible for writing this document, depending on the size of your unit and whether you or a project manager oversaw the project. But you should ensure that it contains complete information and is strong enough to present to the client. Remind your employees to save all relevant copy, emails, receipts, and support documents.

This final report could be anywhere from two to twenty-five pages: don't worry about the length of the report; instead, focus on the value of the content. If you have a lot of support material, such as receipts, memos, or letters of commendation, include them either as a separate document or as an attachment to the report. You can cite them in the report itself.

In terms of content, add whatever you feel is helpful. Most reports contain the standard sections: an overview or a summary with the most important information, especially helpful if the reader is unlikely to peruse the entire document; a list of participants in the project and their specific roles; a brief analysis of the project steps; and financial information.

You may also want to draft a lessons-learned document. It offers a unique opportunity to educate your employees so future projects can be even better. Keep this document short, and make sure all the comments are relevant; don't bother addressing unique or ultimately inconsequential issues. Also, don't name names—stick to processes, tasks, and outcomes and what you have learned from them. Finally, discuss the lessons-learned document at your wrap-up meeting.

Q. Most of my employees are already enmeshed in other projects when another one finally ends. How important is it that they appear for the wrap-up?

A. Actually, the end of the project is when you most need to reconvene. It's critical that you tie up loose ends, discuss any residual points, and bring closure to the project. At this time, employees can also reflect on their good efforts and take a breather—if only for an hour or so.

Q. What if the project ends on a negative note?

A. Occasionally you will have a project that ends badly, so it's even more important that you convene with your team afterward. Otherwise the project, which should serve as a learning experience, can become demoralizing and chaotic. Among other things, get your team together to announce the end. Start by letting them know the reason for the end—and be honest. If your client had specific complaints, they need to hear them for the future. If money ran out, let them know that you, or the project manager, plan to implement better cost management tools in the future. This will preclude any gossip and help your team accept the ending.

Of course, you should also remind them that failure is a part of growth and has much to teach them. Then, list the things the team did accomplish, whether personal or professional, and discuss the lessons learned from the failures and successes. This is also a good time to tie up loose ends and assign closing tasks.

One of those ends will probably be financial. Make sure all the billables are in and that you've accounted for or paid all your bills. If your client is responsible for some of them, such as plane trips and supplies, make sure you sent them along and have an agreement in writing—email will work—that they received and will pay them. If you have any other budget issues, including unaccounted losses, address them. Also, make sure your employees have returned loaned cars, squared away the leases on any warehouses, or returned tools to their original owners. Have anything confidential? Make sure it's stored appropriately.

Q. Is there anything I can do to avoid projects that seem to never end?

A. Remember those goals you or your employees developed early on? Use those as a way of determining whether the project is complete. If you've reached your goals, then you're more or less done. Of course, you probably adapted your list as you went along: the most recent rendition is the one you should use. If you've drafted your goals correctly and accurately, you should be able to avoid this problem altogether.

Q. My team has the same project four times a month, so we just repeat the project management process to varying degrees each time. Because we're always in mid-process, we don't have any significant endings but lots of small ones. Should I still recognize them?

A. Having ongoing beginnings and ends without a break can create burnout and less-than-stellar performances. Employees need to take a breather to replenish themselves. They need to feel good about the work they've done and reflect on ways they could do better in the future. And they need time to receive feedback and, before moving on to other projects, process the information. All endings, even the endings of books, need some kind of wrap-up—for example, an appendix—to truly make the project work.

Appendix

MORE ANSWERS FOR MANAGERS

Here's a list of websites, books, and ideas for answering even more of your questions. These came from the managers and other experts I interviewed for the book and, of course, from me. Let me know if you have other recommendations and I'll post them on my site: http://www.susanfbenjamin.com.

Writing and Communications Issues

- *Chicago Manual of Style* (University of Chicago Press, 15th edition, 2003). Actually, you could also use the Associated Press, Prentice Hall, or other guides. But your department should use a style guide, if only for a reference and to ensure consistency.

- *Eats, Shoots and Leaves* (Gotham, 2003). What's good about Lynn Truss's book is not what you think. Yes, the punctuation rules she discusses are correct, but they won't make you a better writer. The book is entertaining, though, and may trick your employees into thinking that writing is fun.

Forgive me, please—but I had to throw in some of mine:

- *Instant Marketing for Almost Free* (Sourcebooks, 2007). Yes, you do have to market yourself constantly, even if you're managing a team of CPAs. If you need to market a small business, a program within your organization, or just about anything else, all the better.

- *Perfect Phrases for Difficult People at Work* (McGraw Hill, 2007). This book contains exactly what the title says—those perfect phrases to use when managing difficult people.

- *Quick and Painless Business Writing* (Career Press, 2006). In spite of the title, it really is quick and painless—but also informative and fun.

Cultural Issues
- *Culture Shock* (Times Media Private Limited). This almost mile-long series gives you insights into just about every place anyone's ever been, from India to South Africa.

- Mary Beauregard recommends that you read international journals and peruse the web. If you like radio, tune in to the BBC or other shows with a global emphasis.

Disabled Employees
- *Mary Blake passed these along—she said that managers will appreciate the range of content and additional referrals:*

    National Center for Workforce and Disability (http://www.ncwd.gov). This Department of Labor site has plenty of insights for employer and employee.

    Substance Abuse and Mental Health Services Administration's (SAMHSA) National Mental Health Information Center (http://www.mentalhealth.samhsa.gov). This site contains everything from sophisticated content on mental health to practical tips for employers and job seekers.

National Institute of Mental Health (http://www.nimh.nig.gov). Ranges in content from high-level scientific insights to practical tips. Really insightful—the content is as interesting as it is helpful.

To learn more about deaf culture, read these books:

• *Deaf in America: Voices from a Culture* (Harvard University Press, 1st edition, 1998). Carol Padden and Tom Humphries are scholars of language and society and members of the deaf community. Whatever they write on this subject will certainly be important.

• *Train Go Sorry* (Vintage Books, 1995). Leah Hagar Cohen wrote this beautiful memoir about a hearing girl who grew up among deaf children. The book will open your mind *and* be a great read.

If you want to learn American Sign Language, you can buy a book—you'll find plenty out there. But, because signing is all about visual communication, I recommend that you buy a video or, even better, find an American Sign Language teacher and join the class. For a truly worthwhile lesson, make sure the instructor is deaf.

Gender Issues

• *Men Are from Mars, Women Are from Venus* (Quill, 2004). This book is for couples, but the folks I interviewed thought the content was useful at work.
• *Talking 9-5* (William Morrow, 1995). Deborah Tannen's best seller will give you great insights into gender styles at work. A fast, accessible read.

Management Issues

- *Fifth Discipline* (Double Day, 1990). Peter Senge's best seller about creating a learning organization came out in 1990, when many of today's managers were getting nervous about entering junior high school. It has endured and is on lots of managers' must-read lists.

- *Good to Great* (HarperCollins, 2001). Jim Collins and a squad of graduate students looked at various categories of American businesses with top-performing employees. Numerous managers recommend this book.

- *In Search of Excellence* (Profile Business, 2004). Tom Peters and Robert Waterman wrote this business book classic focusing on eight basic principles every manager should know. The case studies are from forty-three companies—all well run and from diverse business sectors. Peters's other classics include *The Pursuit of Wow* and *Thriving on Chaos*.

- *Primal Leadership: Learning to Lead with Emotional Intelligence* (Harvard Business School Press, 2002). Daniel Goldman, Richard E. Boyatzis, and Annie McKee discuss how to lead using core concepts of emotional intelligence.

- *Who Moved My Cheese?* (Putnam, 1998). Spencer Johnson's book about cheese, mice, and managers demonstrates, via the rodent world, how to manage change. A little too cute for some (mice with names like "Sniff" and "Scurry"), but plenty of managers love it.

- *Hope Is Not a Method* (Times Books, 1996). This best seller relays former army chief of staff Gordon Sullivan's experience taking the U.S. Army through enormous change—including entering the information age—and the lessons great managers should know. Written by Sullivan and Michael Harper, it's anecdotal and highly readable.

• *The Revised and Expanded Freakonomics: A Rogue Economist Explores the Hidden Side of Everything* (HarperCollins, 2007). This Stephen Dubner and Steven Levitt book presents, in an eminently readable voice, a new approach to, well, everything.

Hiring, Recruiting, and Other HR Issues

HR Chally Group (http://www.HRchally.com). This website has plenty of helpful answers to HR questions.

Society for Human Resource Management (http://www. shrm.com). The site is a great resource, and for members, it offers a bookstore, regular conferences, and a strong presence in HR-related policy discussion.

American Society for Training and Development (http://www. ASTD.com). Another great organization with book recommendations and lots of answers and ideas.

INDEX

A

accessibility, information, 167–168, 192
active voice, 76–77, 168–169
activities, project, 211–212
ads, employment, 56–57
AFL-CIO Working for America Institute, xii, 68, 158
age, management issues and, 122–125
American Sign Language, 117–118, 229
American Society for Training and Development, 231
Americans with Disabilities Act (ADA), 117
anger, employee, 111–115

B

bad news. *See* negative feedback
Beauregard, Mary, xi, 132, 133
Benjamin, Susan, 227–228, 241–242
Big Brothers/Big Sisters, 127
Blake, Mary, x, 120–121, 228
blogs, 46–47, 133
    company website and, 188–189
body odor, addressing, 100–102
books, 44–46, 133, 163
bosses, 133–137
Boudreau, Martha, x, 45, 132
Boyatzis, Richard E., 230
brainstorming, 32–37
brochures vs. CDs, job fair, 189–190
Bureau of Alcohol, Tobacco, and Firearms (ATF), 174

business writing, 168–173. *See also* language; writing skills

C

calculated risk, 7
CDs vs. brochures, job fair, 189–190
Center for Work-Life Policy, 126
challenge, motivation and, 106
charts, 18–20, 210
    risk management, 27
Chicago Manual of Style, 227
child-rearing issues, 127
citizen groups, 219
clichés, 149
clients
    angry employees and, 111–112
    approval of, documentation, 208
    communicating with, 207
    indecision of, 137–139
    international, 132–133
    preferences, employee, 207
    reluctant, 140–141
clothing, inappropriate, addressing, 100–102
Cohen, Leah Hagar, 229
collaboration, vs. competition, 154
Collins, Jim, 230
communication, 10. *See also* language
    amount of, 13–14
    avoiding, 14–16
    face-to-face vs. virtual, 194–195
    flow, 180–182

ABOUT THE AUTHOR

Host of the talk radio show The Greater Voice, Susan Benjamin has brought business issues to the nation for almost twenty years. Publications from the *Wall Street Journal* to the *Chicago Tribune* have featured Susan's novel approaches while her commentaries on communications-related issues have appeared in newspapers including *USA Today*, the *Miami Herald*, the *Chicago Tribune*, the *New York Daily News*, *Government Executive*, and hundreds of others and are widely distributed through Knight Ridder Tribune.

Susan's books include *Quick and Painless Business Writing* (Career Press, December 2006), *Instant Marketing for Almost Free* (Sourcebooks, January 2007), *Perfect Phrases for Difficult People at Work* (McGraw Hill, September 2007), and *The Top Performer's Guide to Project Management* (Sourcebooks, September 2007), among others.

As a speaker, Susan has appeared on CNN, National Public Radio, and other broadcasts. She has trained over one hundred thousand federal and private sector employees in numerous venues and has given keynote and other addresses. Her clients have included the

Carnegie Mellon Federal Executive Program, the National Geospacial-Intelligence Agency, Liberty Mutual Insurance Group, Fleishman-Hillard International Communications, and many others.

A former professor, Susan mentored academics at Harvard University and MIT. She participated in the White House initiative on Plain Language under the Clinton administration, overseeing the revision of countless documents affecting millions of citizens each year. Her clients included the State Department, Department of Defense, and Food and Drug Administration, as well as hundreds of private sector organizations.

Susan's research includes assessments of organizational communication processes and studies on how language affects reader-responsiveness. Articles about these findings have appeared in publications such as *Scribes Legal Journal*, *Clarity*, *Government Executive*, and *Employment Management Today*.

Susan studied philosophy and writing at Boston University and Bennington College. She received her Masters in Writing from Lesley College, where she worked with C. Michael Curtis, senior editor of the *Atlantic*.

You can find more about Susan at www.thegreatervoice.com and www.susanfbenjamin.com.